23.70

4-28-95

#27186402

FIELD GUIDE TO BUSINESS TERMS

Field Guide to Business Terms: *A Glossary of Essential Tools and Concepts for Today's Manager*

FIELD GUIDE TO BUSINESS TERMS:

A Glossary of Essential Tools and Concepts for Today's Manager

CHIEF CONTRIBUTOR

Tim Hindle

EDITED BY

Alistair D. Williamson

Boston, Massachusetts

97 96 95 94 93   5 4 3 2 1

Field Guide to Business Terms is part of the Harvard Business/The
Economist Reference Book Series and is based on material first published in Great Britain in 1992 by The Economist Books Ltd.

The paper used in this publication meets the requirements of the American National Standard for Performance of Paper for Printed Library
Materials Z39.49-1984.

Library of Congress Cataloging-in-Publication Data

Hindle, Tim.
    Field guide to business terms : a glossary of essential tools and
concepts for today's manager / chief contributor, Tim Hindle ; edited
by Alistair D. Williamson.
        p.   cm. — (Harvard Business/The Economist reference series)
    ISBN 0-97584-434-0 (hard: alk. paper — ISBN 0-87584-412-X (pbk:
    alk. paper)
    1. Industrial management—Terminology.   I. Williamson, Alistair
D.   II. Title.   III. Series.
HD30.17.H56   1993
650'.03—dc20   92-44938
                                                                      CIP

Series design by Mike Fender

CONTENTS

FIELD GUIDE TO BUSINESS TERMS

INTRODUCTION

Field Guide to Business Terms is the first in a new series of books that bring clarity to the often confusing subject of management.

It is written by Tim Hindle, a former management editor of *The Economist,* and is divided into two parts. The first section consists of brief essays, which look at some of the issues that are likely to be at the top of managers' agendas in the 1990s. The bulk of this book consists of a glossary of the main terms that managers use in their everyday working lives but sometimes feel they do not fully understand. The glossary also includes modern jargon words (like just-in-time and IT) and a sprinkling of those foreign words that are becoming part of the language of management, a language that is nevertheless even more firmly based in English than it ever was.

Throughout the glossary are a number of checklists to help managers in their daily business. The book is also sprinkled with quotations from both managers and pundits, showing that management is a broad human endeavor with plenty of room for wit and creativity as well as for triumph and disappointment.

In the glossary, words in SMALL CAPITALS usually indicate a separate entry, thus enabling readers to find other relevant information (though they should note that abbreviations and acronyms are also in capitals).

PART 1

MANAGEMENT IN THE 1990s

Management in the 1990s

ISSUES AND TRENDS

Managers have an identity problem. Most people are confident that they know what economists are and what they do. But a manager can be a lot of things or—some might say—not enough things. One problem is that management is a discipline that embraces a host of others—from computer sciences to law, from psychology to statistics. Nothing is unique to it; it is a sort of academic monster, made up from others' parts.

The enormous growth of MBA (Master of Business Administration) courses in recent years has supplied at least one unintended benefit: It has helped identify the bundle of skills that constitutes management, and it has thus helped young managers feel that at least they know what they should know.

While compiling glossaries that are the core of the books in this series, we found that the problem was not deciding what to include, but what to exclude. "There are few topics that can be regarded as completely useless to managers" begins one recent handbook on the subject. It then goes on to inform its readers, in almost 600 pages, about (among other things) the higher algebra of econometrics and the nature of color blindness.

FOCUSING AWAY FROM THE BLIND SIDE

We, on the other hand, have narrowed our focus somewhat, and color blindness falls outside it. We have decided to be influenced by the fact that management, like everything else, is subject to fashion. The emphasis given to different aspects of it depends on the ethos of the time.

In the 1980s that ethos was dominated by three things in particular.

1. **Following the sun.** There was a fascination in the United States and Europe with unlocking the secrets of the super-successful Japanese. These were seen to lie mostly in their methods of production, in minimizing inventories and work-in-progress, and in introducing "quality management" at all levels of the organization.

2. **The metaphysics of math.** The numerate skills of the accountants and corporate planners who could seemingly create great wealth through takeovers without ever visiting a factory plant or a service point-of-sale.

3. **Globalization.** Driven by the extraordinarily rapid development of telecommunications and computers, by the increasing mobility of capital, and by the harmonization of consumer lifestyles across the developed world, the ability to think and act internationally became crucial. All of a sudden "cultural adaptability" and a second language became essential baggage for every ambitious manager.

For the 1990s we foresee three slightly different dominant features.

1. **Globalization.** This will undoubtedly continue to exert a strong influence on companies for years to come, and foreign

investment is likely to outpace foreign trade as the main vehicle for it. Large companies will lose their national identities as managers work beside colleagues from a host of different nations, and the language of management (still largely English) will come to adopt more expressions from other languages.

2. **Technology.** There are still lessons for managers to learn from the military; from the recent Gulf War came the clear message that today's technology can provide overwhelming competitive advantage. The management of rapidly changing technology will be a key skill for the 1990s. In the service-dominated industries of North America and Western Europe that means information technology in particular.

3. **Management of change.** This is perhaps the biggest challenge for the 1990s. If there has been one discovery in recent years—by companies, their managers, and those who advise them—it is the (perhaps blindingly obvious) fact that all things change. This includes markets, political and economic environments, and the science of management itself.

FUTURE PERFECT: TIMES OF TENSION

This is not to accuse all managers of, until recently, assuming the opposite, but there has been an implicit assumption that things are changing, or being changed, in order to achieve some static state of perfection. The brave who would occasionally admit that such a goal could never be reached would not deny that it existed.

Today that assumption is being abandoned. The rapidly increasing pace of change has brought home to managers the fact that they must live, to some extent, in a state of permanent chaos, a dynamic state that has already been identified by management gurus like Tom Peters. In this world, functions and lines of responsibility are left much less clearly defined.

SOLDIERING ON

To understand what this change means, we need to look back at the history of management, to the military, and to joyless empire builders like Alexander the Great, Hadrian, Genghis Khan, and Napoleon. These men combined the skills of abstract strategy with those of practical logistics. But they thought in static terms. Military campaigns followed the book; and like every good book they had a beginning, a middle, and an end.

The organizational structures needed for the military's finite campaigns were very different from those in the open-ended family around the first recorded housewife. They were authoritarian, with strict rules and hierarchies that sacrificed individual initiative for the benefits of a machine-like efficiency.

OPERATING BY THE BOOK

The Industrial Revolution in Europe and North America grafted these skills onto those of the fifteenth-century Italian book-keepers who had introduced quantitative measurement to the business of business. Factory workers were expected to perform like soldiers; they were given instructions and targets, with no scope to question them. Like soldiers, they were hired for little but their arms and legs.

NEW THOUGHTS

To some degree the science of management since has been a continuing effort to break away from the precision and rigidity inherited from those (inevitably male) soldiers and accountants. A turning point came with the most famous industrial experiment of all time. Known as the Hawthorne Investigation, it started in 1927 at the Western Electric Company's Hawthorne factory in Chicago, and its most famous finding was that workers responded to changes in their physical environment (bright or dim lighting, for example) far less than they responded to the fact that somebody was thinking about their environment. It was the changing of the lighting itself that motivated them, not whether it was bright or dim.

SQUARING THE CIRCLE

The static industrial model of military cohorts neatly arranged for the occasional foray or immediate regrouping is now obsolete everywhere. In today's society of knowledge-workers, management is finding it necessary to emphasize the softer sides of the art—skill and style—at the expense of strategy and structure.

HUMAN RESOURCES

In the 1980s a wide range of companies finally came to believe the old adage about their most valuable resources being their human resources. For many of the decade's fast-growing service companies it was virtually their only resource. Advertising agencies and consulting firms would joke nervously about how all their assets came in and out of the front door every day.

PEOPLE MAKE A DIFFERENCE

With this upgrading of human resources came an upgrading of the personnel function. For many years the personnel department had been a corporate cul-de-sac into which were shunted men and women who had risen above their level of competence. It was often a no-exit career move. But the new-found status of human resources changed that, and with the change came a new name for the personnel job: human resource management.

COMPLICATED SPIRITS . . .

Motivation is at the heart of human resource management, and it is a complex beast. One of the lessons that the increasingly powerful human resource managers learned in the 1980s was that if they spent long hours devising clever pay scales and infinitely subtle bonus schemes, they were largely wasting their time. Money alone could not motivate the right people to stay and to perform better.

Yet for much of the 1980s money was embedding itself more deeply into the reward system. "Performance-related bonus schemes" proliferated. Nobody, however, could find a link between corporate performance and the level (or indeed the existence) of such practices. Some of the highest bonuses were going to managers of the worst companies, and vice versa. Studies suggested that employees who claimed that financial issues were at the root of their discontent were usually hiding a deeper unhappiness with more abstract elements of their working life. It is easier to go to an employer and say, "You are not paying me enough. I'm leaving," than, "This job does not make me feel proud of myself. I'm leaving." This puts a large question mark over pay as the main motivator behind successful companies.

. . . MUST BE UNDERSTOOD BY THEIR PRIORITIES . . .

Awareness of such complexity has made the human resource specialists look back to the 1960s, when the work of men like Abraham Maslow defined a framework for thinking about the psychology of the workplace. Maslow looked at the things that an individual needs as either physiological (like oxygen and water) or psychological (like security and recognition).

These needs come in a definite order of priority, ranked by the length of time that people can do without them. For the physiological needs the order is (from shortest to longest): oxygen, water, food, rest, constant body temperature, and reproduction. The psychological needs Maslow also ranked from shortest to longest: security/self-control, social relationships, self-esteem, status/recognition, achievement/challenge, power, creativity, and self-actualization.

Early items on the list take priority over later ones. So somebody gasping for oxygen is not going to be too concerned about making babies, for example. Similarly, people with no job security (a word whose stem means "without fear") are not going to worry about getting on well with their colleagues at work until they do feel secure. In other words, the firm that hires and fires willy-nilly cannot expect good teamwork.

. . . AND NOT ISOLATED BY MACHINES

This is rather different from the working environment envisaged by management soothsayers a short time ago. A combination of demographic change and new technology was supposed to distance people from each other. In the post-robotic age, motivation and human relationships would count for little. People would no longer work in a huddle on production lines. They would be freed by machines to become knowledge-workers, better educated and better trained. The prime relationship of these knowledge-workers would be with machines—the computer and the telephone—and these would formalize and filter messages between them. People would work independently, from homes deep in the countryside, telecommuting with other workers also deep in the countryside.

In recent years many companies in Europe and the United States did shrink their workforces dramatically. This was not because demographics had created a labor shortage, but because they went to the corporate health farm and there shed some excess fat. But their slimmed-down workforces did not disappear into the solitude of sylvan cottages. To the surprise of many, information technology and robotics increased rather than diminished the value of human contact between workers freed from the mind-numbing tasks that technology had taken over. The independent telecommuters, to whom once in-house tasks were being subcontracted, preferred to stay close to corporate headquarters. The need for social relationships among the new-style knowledge-workers increased. In Maslow's scheme of things that had to be at the expense of creativity and achievement.

THE BOTTOM LINE: WHAT DOES IT MEAN?

Frederick Herzberg, a distinguished professor of management, wrote:

> *Our love affair with numbers is the root cause of the pas-*
> *sionlessness of the 1980s. We try to escape the nihilism of zero by*
> *putting our dreams and emotions into greater and greater num-*
> *bers. How many pieces of information will fit on a computer*
> *chip? How many billions can we add or cut from the budget?*
> *Numbers numb our feelings for what is being counted and lead*
> *to adoration of the economies of scale. Passion is in feeling the*
> *quality of experience, not in trying to measure it.*

Herzberg eloquently represents today's counter-reaction to the authority of the accountants and the number-crunchers who dominated the 1980s. That domination was particularly strong in the United States and in the United Kingdom where a whole generation of top managers had been first trained as accountants. (After World War II accounting was seen as a substitute for a then nonexistent management education.) Senior executives of the 1980s could read a set of accounts very easily, believing that accounts could record precisely the profits of a company in much the same way that they could record the number of widgets coming off the production line. But they could have been led to believe exactly the opposite. Accountants are frequently undecided about the best way to measure things other than widgets. They disguise their doubts by issuing so-called accounting standards on contentious issues like goodwill, extraordinary items, or deferred tax. These standards attempt to dispel the ambiguity that rigorous accountants find uncomfortable.

BUBBLE TROUBLE

Inflation accounting was the one issue that might have alerted businessmen and financiers to the fact that accounts should not be taken too literally. In the late 1970s, when inflation was well into double figures in many developed countries, accountants spent hours tussling with the question of how to cope with it in accounts. There was no doubt that they had a problem. Something that cost $100 at the beginning of a year cost, say, $115 by the end of the year. Mixing nominal values on January 1 with nominal values on December 31 was like adding inches and centimeters.

Various ways of handling this problem were suggested, and eventually accountants settled for one of them. Large companies were instructed to publish inflation-adjusted statements for a three-year experimental period. By 1983, the end of the three years, inflation was way down in single figures, and to their great relief companies were allowed quietly to drop the awkward attempt to take account of changing prices. A precise and unique measurement of profit in a time of inflation had proved to be illusory.

BRAND BALANCING

There were other signs that the emperor of accounting precision was wearing no clothes. For example, the popular new accounting pastime in the late 1980s of valuing "brand names" (intangible assets like Smirnoff or Kit-Kat) produced some extraordinary nonsense. Accountants decided that the value of newly purchased brands could be added to the balance sheet, but not the value of those that had been developed over a number of years. So Smirnoff (plus a few other lesser names bought by Grand Metropolitan in 1987) became worth $500 million, while Gordon's Gin, for example, was not officially worth a penny.

TERMISM — A QUESTION OF ATTITUDES

U.S. and U.K. companies are tempted to make all the little (and sometimes not so little) accounting tweaks that they can to increase reported profits because they are under the constant scrutiny of the stock market, which will hammer ruthlessly any downward kink in the corporate growth curve or any cut in a company's dividend. In Europe, companies' shares are less widely held, and so they worry less about the stock market. They try to smooth out the good years with the bad by sometimes using accounting techniques to actually reduce reported profits.

So accounts are not a clear, precise snapshot of anything. They are more like a picture of the surface of some faraway planet—interesting, but in need of interpretation. Some might see a mountain where others see a crater.

PROFIT MOTIVES

If accounts are imprecise, so too are measures of profit. Is that something to worry about? Yes, if you think that profit is the only measure of corporate virility, but not if you share the view of management writer Charles Handy. He believes that companies are not on this earth primarily to make profits. While an expatriate manager with an oil company, Handy found the slogan that had been above the blackboard in every classroom at his business school—"The purpose of a company is to maximize medium-term earnings [that is, profits] per share"—to be "very remote, very long-term, very intellectual, very unreal." It was no use to him either as a measure of his performance or as a guide to his future behavior.

He maintained that profits were useful merely to make some things possible or to make them more abundantly with better quality. They are a necessary condition for continuing to do business, but they are not sufficient alone, and they never will be.

TERRIFIED OF IT?

It took a long time for the machinery of information technology—computers and advanced telecommunications—to reach the offices of senior and middle managers. Now that they have arrived, however, they have already started revolutionizing the way that companies work.

RISING FROM THE DEPTHS

Computers crept into the corporation gradually. At first, huge mainframes were shut up in vast, dingy basements, whirring away at night and supervised by a pallid breed of night watchman known as a computer manager.

Unlike humans, as computers grew up, they grew smaller. As they shrank in size, they moved upstairs from the basement and into different departments—finance, stock control, and so forth. They moved first to departments where their expense could most easily be justified in terms of the manpower that it saved. Only in government organizations, like census departments and tax authorities where monumental tasks of paper processing were threatening to strangle them into irreversible coma, were they accepted more widely and more quickly.

ON TO THE FACTORY FLOOR

In time, with the development of robotics, computers moved on to the factory floor. Fiat, the Italian car manufacturer, saw extensive use of robots as the only way for European manufacturers to compete with the Japanese. They would reduce to a minimum the need for Italian labor, whose expectations were so far above those of Japanese workers that they could not hope to produce competitively priced products.

SLOWLY TO THE TOP

This piecemeal development left companies with a number of "islands" of IT in far-flung areas such as design, accounting, and manufacturing. Senior managers who could not justify IT for themselves on any normal cost-benefit analysis were left at sea. A 1988 survey by the Massachusetts Institute of Technology

(MIT) estimated that no more than 10–15% of senior executives in large American companies had computers on their desks, and no more than half of them were using their computers properly.

Since then computers have gradually appeared on the chief executive's desk for a number of reasons.

1. They started to be more "executive friendly." Led by Apple, computer manufacturers developed a range of machines that eliminated the trauma of sending the over-50s off for typing lessons.

2. A common phenomenon of the 1980s—the streamlining of company headquarters—left executives with fewer support staff. They saw computers as a possible replacement for that disappearing support.

3. They also saw that the economic world around them was changing unmanageably fast. There was no longer any permanence to interest or exchange rates; new products came and went as quickly as the seasons. There was no way to keep up to date with the impact these changes were having on their businesses if they continued to use old-style paper-based reporting systems. As a "pre-tech exec," the boss of Rank Xerox used to receive regular reports the size of telephone directories. After he took to the computer these were whittled down to five on-screen pages.

LINKING UP

Once the corporate sea was filled with islands of IT, companies wanted to combine the islands into a single unit. Telecommunications then came into its own, linking computers in one part of the organization with those in another. This "networking" allowed all parts of the organization (at home and abroad) to have access to huge amounts of information that they had never before imagined would be available to them.

Naturally this made senior managers nervous. They understood as well as any petty potentate in the Dark Ages that information is power. And was not power their exclusive monopoly?

OPENING UP . . .

They became even more nervous when they allowed themselves to contemplate the future of telecommunications. They were being told that the development of fiber optics would cause an explosion in telecommunications capacity. Arthur Andersen, the leading consultant in IT, prophesied that before the end of the 1990s, 10 million conversations would be carried simultaneously by a single fiber optic, compared with 3,000 in the late 1980s. That should definitely do something dramatic to the price of telecommunications. It should also destroy one of the main arguments for not disseminating information more widely throughout companies. "We are moving towards the capability to communicate anything to anyone, anywhere, by any form— voice, data, text or image—at the speed of light," predicted John Naisbett and Patricia Aburdene in their bestseller *Megatrends 2000*.

The future capability of telecommunications threatens to change the function of management in the corporations of the future. For a start, its job will no longer be deciding which information to filter to which department; all information will be available to everybody. The manager's task will be to make it meaningful, and then to act accordingly. This does not imply that companies will need fewer managers, but they will require better-trained managers who can understand what the messages that they are receiving about their external environment (and about their company) mean.

. . . AND INFORMATING

An expression has arisen to describe this new phenomenon: IT is not "automating" management; it is, rather, "informating" it. Automating makes humans redundant; informating makes them even more valuable.

Shoshana Zuboff, a professor of business administration at

Harvard, is a leading proponent of the theory of the "informated" as opposed to the "automated" company. In one interview she described clearly what she believes is involved in this process:

> Throughout history technology has been designed to substitute for the human body and do the same things only faster, with less or no human intervention, at lower cost. Over the past few decades this logic has come to be known as automation. The assumption is that more automation means higher productivity. The more technology you have, the fewer people you need. . . . In my research, however, I observed that these rules about automation did not hold true for information technology. The introduction of computer technology did not necessarily mean you could get by with fewer, less intelligent people.
>
> With a technology that informates, you start to have masses and masses of data that hold all the riches, all the opportunities to learn something about the business that never could have been learned before. The business and its various dynamics become transparent, and this transparency is the new source of wealth of the company. This brings us to the second meaning of informating. It is about the strategic intent of the firm, and implies a profoundly different conception of organization and management. Informating represents the changing distribution of knowledge, authority and power. It means that the new purpose and function of management is the fusing of work and learning. Unfortunately, under the automation paradigm the people on the front lines are not trained to understand information or to do anything with it. Control of most information still rests in upper management's hands.

Stimulating stuff, which in essence seems to say that managers should not be afraid of IT. It will not automate their jobs away. In fact, it will do quite the opposite: it should informate them to new heights of fulfillment.

PART 2

GLOSSARY

Acceptance credit

A **BILL OF EXCHANGE** that has been endorsed by a bank; that is, the bank has given its guarantee that the bill will be paid. This is a popular way of financing trade between buyers and sellers who do not know each other but who do trust each other's bank. The bank charges a fee for its endorsement. Sellers who have a bill "accepted" by a reputable bank can then sell the bill (at a **DISCOUNT**) and get immediate payment for the goods they have sold.

Accounting firms

Once upon a time there used to be eight big accounting firms called the "Big Eight." They audited the books of over 80% of the world's largest companies. Then these accounting firms began to branch out into a more lucrative and faster-growing line of business: **MANAGEMENT** consulting. This forced the Big Eight to spread around the globe in pursuit of their firms' multinational clients.

The firms grew bigger and bigger, but since they had traditionally been set up as **PARTNERSHIPS**, the additional demands on their **CAPITAL** burdened them. To overcome this problem they began to merge with each other, and the Big Eight became the Big Six. One survey by the Center for International Financial Analysis and Research (CIFAR) came up with the following figures for the Big Six in 1990.

Firm	Big Companies Audited	Offices
Ernst & Young	3,231	777
KPMG Klynveld Peat Marwick Goerdeler	3,163	864
Deloitte Ross Tohmatsu	2,726	722
Coopers & Lybrand	2,380	737
Price Waterhouse	1,691	496
Arthur Andersen	1,627	289

There is a continual problem of people not leaving.

Senior Partner, KPMG

ACCOUNTING STANDARDS

When accountants are uncertain about how to VALUE particular items in companies' accounts, their professional associations get together to rule on what they consider to be "best practice." This advice is issued in the form of accounting standards. Some controversial areas that the associations have tried to rule on include accounting for INFLATION, for foreign-currency conversion, for deferred tax, and for GOODWILL.

Different countries give their standards different weight. In Canada they have legal backing; in the United States they are compulsory for companies registered with the SECURITIES AND EXCHANGE COMMISSION (SEC); and in the United Kingdom they are voluntary. Any COMPANY not following them has to explain why.

ACCOUNTS PAYABLE

See CREDITOR

Accounts receivable

See DEBTOR

Acid test

Also known as the "quick ratio," this is the ratio of a COM-PANY's liquid ASSETS (like cash, bank balances, and easily salable SECURITIES) to its short-term debts, that is, the money it must repay other people in the not-too-distant future. It is widely used by financial analysts and bankers to determine whether a company has sufficient LIQUIDITY.

Acquisition

The purchase of a controlling interest in one COMPANY by another; popularly linked with mergers through the expression M&A (short for mergers and acquisitions). Acquisitions can be friendly (when both companies agree to the purchase) or hostile (when some shareholders sell out to the buyer against the wishes of MANAGEMENT and other shareholders). Whatever form they take, acquisitions are rarely without pain for both the acquirer and the acquired.

Added value

Or "VALUE-added," the difference between what a COMPANY spends buying materials from outside and what it receives from selling its products. Out of this added value the firm has to pay wages, rent, and interest. The rest is PROFIT.

Calculating the added value at different stages of the production process can help a company identify the most profitable parts of its business. It may show that certain processes would be cheaper if brought in from outside. In the COMPUTER and textile industries, for example, semifinished products are shipped halfway across the world (and then back again) for LABOR-intensive processes to be carried out in places where labor is much cheaper.

ADVERTISING

The glamorous part of **MARKETING**, in which a firm's products and **SERVICES** are fulsomely described in newspaper announcements, billboards, or in short films shown on television. The heart of the advertising industry is on Madison Avenue in New York. It passed briefly to London in the 1980s.

Advertising aims to inform **CONSUMERS** about products. It may also entertain them in the process. The only guarantee that it is not misleading is the advertising industry's own sanctions against its members.

David Ogilvy (founder of the Ogilvy & Mather advertising agency, now part of the WPP Group) once gave 16 tips on television advertising. They are hard to beat.

- Identify the brand and make it memorable. Use its name within the first 10 seconds; then play word games with it, or spell it out.
- Show the product and its packaging.
- If advertising food, show it in motion. Pour syrup over pancakes. Do not let it just sit there.
- Use close-ups.
- Start with a bang. If you only finish with a bang, your audience will not see it. They will be busy getting a snack.
- If you do not have much to say, put it in song, but make sure audiences can understand the words of your jingle.
- Sound effects can be very powerful—bacon sizzling or coffee percolating, for example.
- Try to have actors talking on camera rather than voice-overs.
- Reinforce your message by superimposing it in type as the soundtrack speaks the words.
- Avoid the visually banal—the happy family at the breakfast table, for example.
- Do not change scenes too often. Too many changes can be very confusing.

- Use a mnemonic, a visual device that is repeated again and again, like MGM's roaring lion.

- Show the product in use: the car on the road, the beer being drunk.

- Do not forget that anything is possible on television. Let your imagination rip.

- Make sure that advertisements are crystal clear. (Ogilvy claimed that more than half the commercials he saw were incomprehensible.)

- Television commercials are very expensive. There is no research to prove it, but Ogilvy suspected that there is a negative correlation between the money spent on producing a television advertisement and its ability to sell a product.

AFFILIATE

A COMPANY, X, that is partly owned by another company, Y, is said to be an affiliate of Y and of all Y's other affiliates. Because of their relationship, affiliates' dealings with each other are not always ARM'S-LENGTH commercial transactions.

The word "affiliate" can also refer to noncorporate entities that have close links. For example, individual TRADE UNIONS are "affiliated" to their central organization.

(See also ASSOCIATED COMPANY, SUBSIDIARY)

AGENCY

The relationship between principal and AGENT is one that pervades the whole of the business world. An agent is given power by a principal to act on its behalf. In return, an agent must always act with due care and in the principal's best interest.

Stockbrokers act as agents, buying and selling SHARES on behalf of their clients, the principals. Advertising agencies, EMPLOYMENT AGENCIES, shipping agencies, and so on, are at every corner of a businessperson's life.

An agency relationship that is not immediately recognized is that between the shareholders of a **PUBLIC COMPANY** (the principals) and the company's directors and managers (the shareholders' agents). One theory has it that many of the failings of public companies today are due to the shortcomings of this relationship (variously known as the agency problem or the agency theory).

Managers and directors (as agents) are obliged to look after the best interests of their principals. Yet in practice they do not, and in theory they cannot. In practice, managers inevitably put their own interests first. And this is not always such a visibly gross excess as a personalized jet for the chief executive. As responsibility is delegated down through the organization, the intervention of personal interests is bound to dilute the primacy of shareholders more and more.

Take a step back and ask a question: "What is the best interest of the principals?" One common answer is "The long-term maximization of shareholder wealth." But as a theoretical aim for most managers that is useless. How then are managers to act as agents if they do not recognize the best interests of their principals?

Agent

A central figure in most businesses, the agent is a **COMPANY** or individual with the authority to carry out transactions with third parties on behalf of somebody else (called "the principal"). Agents are frequently used to buy or sell goods in remote or inaccessible **MARKETS**.

Sole agent. Somebody with an exclusive agreement to be the only person (or company) allowed to buy or sell on behalf of the principal in a particular geographic region.

Commission agent. An agent who is rewarded by a commission, that is, an agreed percentage of the **VALUE** of the goods that she buys or sells.

In one sense managers are "agents" of a company's shareholders. Some see the shortcomings of this agency relationship as one of the central failings of capitalism.

ALLIANCE

The joining together of two corporations (often competitors) in a loose link for what they see as being their mutual benefit. Thus AT&T, the telecommunications company, and Olivetti, the Italian COMPUTER company, formed an alliance that involved AT&T buying 25% of Olivetti and both sides promising to develop a lot of new business together in the fast-growing field of INFORMATION TECHNOLOGY. The alliance, however, proved disappointing to both sides, and AT&T sold its stake. Undaunted, AT&T has formed at least a half-dozen other strategic alliances with computer and telecommunications companies in Europe and Japan.

AMORTIZATION

See DEPRECIATION

ANALYST

In general, a person who is employed to study some particular feature of the organization. Nowadays two types of analysts feature strongly in the life of the corporation.

Investment analyst. These are the bright young sparks in brokerage firms who demand information about public companies from their managers, churn it about, and then show MANAGEMENT what a lousy job it is doing. A number of companies find that being answerable to investment analysts is one of the most onerous duties of being a PUBLIC COMPANY.

Systems analyst. These are the people responsible for designing, installing, and operating corporate COMPUTER systems. In the early days of the computer, they were a breed apart. They spoke a language more obscure than the white-coated R&D technicians, and they had an arrogance that came from having the power to hold the whole corporation at ransom. As computers have grown smaller, and managers have become more familiar with them, the awesome power of the systems analyst has declined.

ANNUAL GENERAL MEETING

The gathering of shareholders that most companies are legally obliged to hold once a year. The annual general meeting provides a rare opportunity for shareholders to meet and question those who run their COMPANY for them (MANAGEMENT). In practice these meetings are usually tame affairs. Everybody tries hard not to offend; shareholders agree to the DIVIDEND payment and to the reappointment of the AUDITORS; and then everybody heads for the drinks and cocktail sausages. If the company makes CONSUMER goods, the shareholders will expect to take some free samples home at the end of the day.

On the rare occasions that annual general meetings become lively, it is usually because the company has been targeted by an activist group. For many years Barclays Bank's meeting was frequented by vocal antiapartheid groups because of the bank's considerable investment in South Africa. The CONGLOMERATE Hanson had its annual general meeting disturbed by Navajo Indians objecting to the pillage of their lands (as they saw it) by Peabody Coal, America's biggest coal-mining company and a SUBSIDIARY of Hanson.

If shareholders do not take annual general meetings seriously, then top management becomes answerable to nobody but itself. Shareholders should not then be surprised to find themselves financing fleets of cars and jets and the building of self-aggrandizing glass palaces called "headquarters."

ANNUAL PERCENTAGE RATE

Often abbreviated to APR, a standard way of expressing the rate of interest on any form of credit. It is the rate that a flow of interest payments would represent if they were all paid as a single annual payment. The formula is

$$\text{APR} = \frac{100 \times (1 + \text{rate})^n - 100}{100}$$

where n is the number of payments per year.

It is often a legal requirement that all loans offered to the general public show their APR. This is to frustrate loan sharks who want to advertise a rate of interest of "only 10%," when what they mean is 10% per month.

ANNUAL REPORT

The official document sent to a COMPANY'S shareholders informing them of the company's activities in the previous year. The report must, by law, contain certain things.

- An audited copy of the BALANCE SHEET and income statement
- The AUDITORS' report on the statements
- The DIRECTORS' report on the past year's performance
- Consolidated accounts where the company owns a SUBSIDIARY

Other information is often provided voluntarily.

- The chairman's report, a not always unintentionally vague statement of where the company is hoping to go
- A CASH-FLOW statement, which records money coming in and money going out
- A geographical and sectoral breakdown showing where sales and profit came from
- A table of the company's five- or ten-year track record

Many large companies would like to turn their annual reports into coffee-table books. As a rule, the less information provided, the more colorful and thick the report. The 1989 report of Guinness, the British brewing company, contained a list of the names of 14 photographers who had worked on the report. That could stand in the company's own Book of Records.

ANTIDUMPING

Action taken by a government or governments to counteract the "dumping" of goods on their territory by another country. Dumping is the selling of goods in a foreign MARKET, either at a price that is below cost or at a lower price than in the manufacturer's home market.

Antidumping measures can take the form of either import duties, whose purpose is to raise the price of the goods being dumped, or an agreement between the importing country and the manufacturing country to restrict the amount of goods imported at the low price.

Dumping is less easy to identify in practice than in theory. Exported goods may genuinely be cheaper at their point-of-sale than in their home market because of efficient distribution and retailing systems in the importing country. In any case, selling goods at below cost is a valid MARKETING STRATEGY for the launch of a new product, or for the purpose of acting as a "come-on" for other goods and SERVICES (a LOSS LEADER).

Antidumping became a hot issue in the 1980s, with the EUROPEAN COMMUNITY and the United States frequently accusing Japanese and other Far Eastern manufacturers of dumping goods on their markets. A number of cases went for adjudication to the GATT in Geneva. In 1987 the European Commission imposed antidumping duties on photocopiers manufactured in Japan. This had at least three peculiar consequences.

1. European CONSUMERS have since paid a great deal more for their photocopiers than they would otherwise have done.

2. Many Japanese companies have been forced to invest in expensive production facilities inside Europe.

3. The main beneficiary of the duties has been a U.S. COMPANY (Xerox), not a local European company.

ANTITRUST LAWS

This legislation, first passed in 1890, made it illegal to set up monopolies harmful to competition and to act in restraint of trade—by operating a CARTEL, for example.

The antitrust laws have been a powerful weapon against both industrial concentration and the exploitation of monopolies. One of the first companies to become a victim of the legislation was National Cash Register (NCR), which in 1912 was successfully prosecuted for its aggressive MARKETING tactics. John Patterson, its chairman at the time, said that he believed "the best way to kill a dog is to cut off its head."

The EC and many other countries operate strict antitrust laws to combat monopolies and cartels.

APPRAISAL

A systematic way of assessing the performance of employees. Until recently appraisal schemes were part of the process of deciding on promotions, pay raises, or training needs. They only occurred at times of discrete change in an employee's career.

With the popularity of performance-related pay, appraisal schemes have become more like an integral part of everyday decisions about pay itself. Typically they consist of an annual INTERVIEW with a senior manager. At the interview, targets are set against which future performance can be measured. Here are some points the appraiser should remember.

- Be prepared: give advance notice, allow adequate time, and ensure privacy.
- It is a two-way process.
- Review performance, not personality.
- Ask open questions.
- Listen to the answers.

- Review the past and plan the future.
- Agree on development needs and actions to be taken as a result.
- Encourage open, honest discussion.

APPRENTICESHIP

The period served by an apprentice, that is, somebody who signs a CONTRACT with an employer to work for a given period of time (usually for a nominal wage) in return for which the employer agrees to train the apprentice in a particular skill. The professions (medicine, accountancy, and the law) used to have apprenticeship systems, but new recruits into these professions today generally arrive fully fledged, expecting to be fully paid.

Germany has a highly developed apprenticeship system. Some 40% of all young people there receive vocational TRAINING. This combines part-time work with classroom education at special state-run vocational training centers. It is one reason for the high number of Germans with technology and engineering qualifications, and for the high quality of German technology.

APR

See ANNUAL PERCENTAGE RATE

ARBITRAGE

This is the practice of buying a commodity or currency in one MARKET in order to sell it almost immediately in another, instantly profiting from the price differences between the two. In effect, arbitrage smoothes out imperfections between different parts of a market.

Whenever arbitrage takes place, it reduces the opportunity for further arbitrage. Suppose there is an inconsistency in the exchange rates of the yen, the Swiss franc, and the dollar: somebody makes a profit by selling yen for Swiss francs in Tokyo, using the francs to buy dollars in Geneva, before selling the dollars for yen in New York. (Such a person will, of course, have to buy and sell in large quantities in order to ensure that the dealing charges on the transactions do not eat up all the PROFIT.)

In the 1980s the word encompassed dealings in stocks and SHARES, where it was sometimes referred to as risk arbitrage. "Arbitrageurs" (commonly known as "arbs") were people who bought the shares of companies that they suspected were about to be the subject of a takeover bid (or bought the right to buy such shares at an agreed price in the future). Since a bid would automatically push up the price of these shares, arbs could subsequently sell them at a profit.

Arbs were considered disreputable because they frequently acted with the benefit of inside information on the fate of the company in question. Such "insider trading" is illegal in many countries, and a number of arbs ended up in jail.

ARBITRATION

An alternative procedure to the courts for settling commercial disputes. Those in disagreement (over, say, the terms of a CONTRACT) turn to an independent third party whose judgment they have agreed in advance to accept to settle the problem. The third party (the arbitrator) may be a panel of experts, in which case one of them will be appointed to make the final decision. An arbitrator's judgment is known as an "award."

Several international bodies (including the GATT and some international industry associations) have set up arbitration systems to help settle international commercial disputes.

There are a number of advantages to arbitration.

- Going through the courts can be long, drawn out, and expensive, especially when it involves more than one jurisdiction.
- The parties to the dispute can choose as arbitrator someone who not only knows the law but who also knows their own specialist business.

- The process can take place in secret, which is valuable when companies are arguing about commercially sensitive matters.
- The venue and timing of the process are much more flexible than with a judge and court attendants.
- Even when committed to arbitration, the parties involved do not necessarily give up their right to subsequently take the case to court.

ARM'S-LENGTH

A transaction is said to be done "at arm's-length" if it is carried out between a totally unrelated buyer and seller. If the buyer and seller are in some way related (first cousins, or a holding COMPANY and its SUBSIDIARY), then the price they agree on might be affected by factors that would not apply in a totally free market.

Tax authorities zealously investigate to confirm that transactions between related companies are carried out at arm's-length. Otherwise, by means of TRANSFER PRICING, large groups can easily avoid paying huge taxes.

ASSEMBLY LINE

This is a system of manufacturing—revolutionary in its time— in which the product comes to the worker instead of the worker coming to the product. An article moves along a line to workers (called a "station"), each of whom adds some part of assembly before it passes on to the next worker. Ultimately the finished product drops off at the end of the line.

One problem with assembly-line production is that unless each station's task takes exactly the same amount of time, the operation is inefficient. Workers can be left idle while a process is completed farther up the line. This problem can be overcome by using robots programmed for identical lengths of time for each assembly-line procedure.

ASSESSMENT CENTER

More a process than a place, this is a series of tests and INTER-VIEWS with job candidates that can stretch over a number of days. It is basically an attempt to improve on the more normal method of job selection based on a single sheet of qualifications (the candidate's resume) and a short interview.

ASSETS

Anything that a COMPANY (or an individual) owns that can be given a monetary VALUE, including intangible things like GOODWILL.

A company's assets are listed on the left-hand side of its BAL-ANCE SHEET, except in the United Kingdom where the LIABILI-TIES (like the traffic) tend to go on the left. They are further divided into FIXED ASSETS (which are not easy to move) and CUR-RENT ASSETS (which are).

Assets are notorious for being stripped. "Asset stripping" is a financially sophisticated sleight-of-hand that relies on the fact that the value of the assets on a company's balance sheet (net of its liabilities) is sometimes higher than the value of its SHARES on the STOCK MARKET. Under those circumstances a so-called asset stripper can make a successful bid for the company's shares, sell off all its assets, and be left with a tidy PROFIT. Asset strippers are not considered to be of great value to industrial society.

No one has a greater asset for his business than a man's pride in his work.

Mary Parker Follett

ASSOCIATED COMPANY

Company A is an associated COMPANY of Company B if more than 20%, but less than 50%, of its EQUITY is owned by Company B. This makes the relationship between the two companies less than that between a holding company and its SUBSIDIARY. It is a more significant relationship than that between an ordinary investor and the company in which the investor holds SHARES.

Companies do not need to consolidate associated companies in their accounts unless they CONTROL the composition of the BOARD of directors of the associated company, in which case it is deemed to be a subsidiary.

AUDIT/AUDITOR

Almost everywhere, it is a requirement that a company's accounts be inspected and checked by an outside independent firm of recognized accountants or by a special government body set up for the purpose. This inspection is called an audit, and the inspectors are called auditors.

Auditing is an old business; the word is derived from the Latin for hearing. In olden days, it referred to the "hearing" that the owner of land gave to the manager in which the manager would account for his stewardship. Nowadays auditors are appointed by shareholders and report to them. Their report may be either "clean" or "qualified." It will be qualified if the auditors have been unable to satisfy themselves on any issue that they are legally obligated to check. Companies go to great lengths to avoid the stigma of a qualified audit.

An auditor's main concern is to see whether the accounts represent a "true and fair view" of the company's affairs. "True and fair" is the central principle of accounting, and there is a general assumption that there is only one true and fair view of things. But accountants can (and do) easily disagree about what is true and about what is fair, so any audit that is deemed clean by one reputable accountant could truly and fairly be qualified by another.

In recent years the word has taken on a wider meaning. Companies have "internal audits," that is, inspections of the accounts carried out by a committee or individual from inside the business. And they have "environmental audits" to check that the company is complying with environmental legislation and doing what it can to avoid pollution. Next will come "human resource audits."

AUFSICHTSRAT

The supervisory **BOARD**, mandatory for the many German companies that must have two boards: a supervisory board and a **MANAGEMENT** board (*VORSTAND*). Members of the *Aufsichtsrat* are elected by shareholders, and one of their main responsibilities is the election of members of the *Vorstand.*

AUTOMATION

The process of replacing human **LABOR** with machines. Early automation aroused strong reactions. The Luddites, who were a group of nineteenth-century workers, willfully destroyed **FACTORY** machines in the north of England on the grounds that they took away their livelihood. Their name has gone into the dictionary.

Modern automation has focused on **ROBOTICS**, the use of **COMPUTER**-driven robots to perform industrial tasks with an absolute minimum of human intervention. Robotics has been widely introduced into the car industry and has on occasion aroused emotions only slightly less negative than the Luddites'.

INFORMATION TECHNOLOGY, the combination of telecommunications and **COMPUTERS**, is seen by some as the first form of automation that does not threaten human labor. The argument is that the wider dissemination of information throughout corporations (which is the consequence of information technology) requires more (and better) human intervention in order to interpret and make use of it for the benefit of the corporation.

It was naive of nineteenth-century optimists to expect paradise from technology, and it is equally naive of twentieth-century pessimists to make technology the scapegoat for such old shortcomings as man's blindness, cruelty, immaturity, greed and sinful pride.

Peter Drucker

AVERAGE COST

This method is perhaps the most logical way to value stocks (inventory) for the purpose of finding out the full COST of manufacturing a single item. Average cost is the total cost of manufacturing all the inventory held by a COMPANY divided by the number of units held.

In practice, accountants prefer to value stocks on the LAST IN, FIRST OUT or FIRST IN, FIRST OUT principle. This is partly because average cost has to be complicatedly recalculated every time a unit is added or taken away from the inventory. But it is also because both LIFO and FIFO give real costs that have actually been paid for particular units of inventory. Most accountants prefer to work with sums that have actually been paid for things, rather than with theoretical calculations that never were. (See also STATISTICS)

Back-up

The essential business of having a **COMPUTER** system make copies of data that are being stored in it. Despite the marvels of modern silicon technology, it is still as easy (if not easier) to lose a computer file as it is to lose a paper one. More often the loss is the result of human error, but there are still occasions when computer files disappear into thin air for what can only be termed "technological reasons."

Bad debt

Debts come in three standard shapes and an infinite number of sizes. The shapes are as follows:

Good. There is no reason to believe the debt will not be repaid on time.

Doubtful. It looks as if the debt might not be repaid.

Bad. The debt appears to be irrecoverable, or it would cost more to recover it than the debt is worth.

All debts are born good, some then prove doubtful, and (hopefully) only a few become bad. Bad debts can be seen as the price paid by all businesses for the benefit of **LIMITED LIABILITY**. The nature of really successful business is **RISK**, so few companies are entirely free of them. The trick is to keep them at an accountable level.

Good debts appear as an asset on a **COMPANY'S BALANCE SHEET**. If the company needs the cash represented by the debts in a hurry, it can "factor" them to a finance business. Firms offering a **FACTORING** service buy the debts at a **DISCOUNT** from the **CREDITOR**. They then set about collecting the money from the debtors, taking a risk that they will collect at least as much as they have paid for the debts.

As debts change shape, their treatment in the creditor's accounts changes. Provisions (a percentage of the total value of the debt) have to be set aside out of **PROFITS** against debts that become doubtful. The creditor then has to make a judgment as to whether to pursue the debt through the courts (and risk bankrupting the **DEBTOR** and getting nothing at the end of the day) or to be patient in the hope that the debtor can eventually pay in full. Bad debts must be written off in the accounts as a loss; in other words the whole amount has to be deducted from profits.

BALANCE OF PAYMENTS

The closely observed accounts of a country's trade with the rest of the world; the record of its external payments (and receipts). Since one country's payment must be another's receipt, it is not unreasonable to assume that the sum of every nation's balance of payments should be zero. But it is not. There is a consistent world deficit of tens of billions of dollars.

This is not because of the world's trade with Mars, but the result of difficulties in measuring trade.

The balance of payments is generally divided into two types.

Capital account. This records flows of **CAPITAL**: long-term investments (like **COMPANY** A buying foreign company B) and short-term investments (like cash searching for a higher rate of return in a foreign currency). As more and more countries remove exchange-control regulations, these hard-to-measure flows are multiplying.

Current account. This records trade in goods (visible trade) and **SERVICES** (invisible trade). Trade in services—things like tourism, income from foreign investment and banking—is growing much faster than trade in goods. It is much more difficult to measure this invisible trade, however, than the traditional trade in widgets. So inaccuracies in the current account are likely to increase in the future, which will be of no help to the world's persistent deficit.

BALANCE SHEET

The statement of a **COMPANY'S ASSETS** and **LIABILITIES**. The balance sheet and the income statement are the backbone of a company's annual report, the yearly account of a company made by the managers of a company to its owners.

The balance sheet is a sort of snapshot of the worth of a company at close of business on one particular day. It is a blurred snapshot, however, for several reasons. Some assets cannot be valued by accountants, so they do not appear on the balance sheet. **EUROPEAN COMMUNITY** legislation has introduced a standard format for balance sheets across Europe, but it will be some time before different countries' accounts are sufficiently similar for valid cross-country comparisons to be widely made. For the moment, one cannot assume that an Italian's assets are equal to anybody else's.

BANKER'S DRAFT

A useful way of financing trade between two parties who do not know each other, a banker's draft is a sort of check written by a bank on itself. A **DEBTOR** buys one from a bank and gives it to its **CREDITOR** when the creditor will not accept the debtor's own check. Assuming that the bank itself is not about to go bust, a banker's draft is as good as cash.

The banker's draft provides a vivid example of the way in which banks make money out of people's distrust of each other. When companies have more trust in, say, IBM than they have in their bank, they begin to cut their bank out of their business, a process that is called "disintermediation."

If you owe your bank £100, you have a problem. But if you owe it £1 million then it has.

John Maynard Keynes

BANKRUPTCY

The condition of being bankrupt. A DEBTOR becomes bankrupt when the courts agree to his request (or that from an unpaid CREDITOR) to be declared insolvent, that is, unable to pay debts when they become due. The courts then appoint an official to assess the bankrupt person's ASSETS and LIABILITIES and to apportion them (apart from clothing and the tools of his trade) to his creditors.

When this has been completed to the court's satisfaction the bankruptcy will be discharged. Until that time, such people are known as "undischarged bankrupts." There are tight restrictions on what undischarged bankrupts may do.

BAR CHART

A simple graphical way of representing a series of data that measure the same element under different circumstances—for example, the maximum temperature in different countries, or the average COST of living in different large cities. The bar chart and the PIE CHART are the most commonly used charts in business.

BAR CODING

The vertical lines of differing thicknesses that appear on the packaging of most products today. Bar codes enable electronic scanners at the POINT-OF-SALE to read several details about the product (including its price), thus saving the time of the cashier having to key anything manually. Bar coding is also helpful in stock CONTROL.

BARRIER TO ENTRY

An obstacle to entry into a MARKET that occurs naturally: for example, only one firm can get the best site for selling a particular product. A hypermarket may pay a high price for a field near a new highway intersection simply to prevent rivals from acquiring it as much as to get it for itself.

Other natural barriers arise because established firms benefit from ECONOMIES OF SCALE that the newcomer cannot hope to reap immediately. Newcomers also have to overcome customer loyalty to well-established firms in the business.

Artificial barriers to entry are erected by existing firms in a market to discourage new competition. Market leaders can cut prices, maybe even below cost for a period, to make the newcomer's entry extra difficult.

Barriers to entry are closely watched by antitrust authorities. While in most cases they are perfectly legitimate competitive behavior, in extremis they can constitute what is known as "an abuse of a dominant position."

BARRIER TO EXIT

An obstacle discouraging a firm from getting out of a MARKET in which it is making little or no PROFIT. In some cases one firm's BARRIER TO ENTRY can be another's barrier to exit. If a firm increases production and advertising to raise the hurdle that the new market entrant must climb to get in, these same (expensive) measures may discourage that firm from getting out should its competitive STRATEGY not pay off.

Past costs that have to be written off can act as a barrier to exit. So too can COSTS yet to be incurred. For example, compensation may have to be paid to get out of long-term contractual obligations. And severance payments for unwanted workers can be expensive. Last, and by no means least, there is the fear of being seen to fail, the factor that more than any other keeps companies in business long after all signals warn them to run for the exit.

BARTER

The direct exchange of goods for other goods, a form of trading that is at least as old as money itself. Barter is unpopular with banks because it reduces the need for their SERVICES, but it is often popular with businesses. They can use it to avoid taxes if the goods are not converted into their monetary VALUE (and hence do not pass through the income statement). Tax authorities, naturally, demand that all barter deals be converted for accounting purposes. (See also COUNTERTRADE)

BATCH

A bunch of things that have something in common. The word is used commercially in such phrases as the following:

Batch processing. The gathering of COMPUTER data in batches before they are processed, that is an alternative to processing each bit of data singly (and inefficiently) as and when it is ready.

Batch production. A method of manufacturing things in batches that falls somewhere between MASS PRODUCTION and handicraft. Batch production fails to glean the advantages of mass production (such as ECONOMIES OF SCALE) and needs to be costed in a special way.

BEARER BOND

A BOND that belongs to whoever "bears" it (whoever has the bond document in hand) in contrast to normal bonds whose rightful owner is registered with the issuer of the bond. A bearer bond usually comes with a book of coupons attached. The coupons are handed in on their due dates in order to claim the interest payments on the bond.

Bonds issued in the EUROMARKET are always issued in bearer form. They have the great MARKETING advantage of being virtually untraceable by tax inspectors.

BIG BANG

The change that occurred on October 27, 1986, when the London Stock Exchange threw out many of its restrictive practices, including the strict separation between dealers ("jobbers") and agents ("brokers"). The biggest bang on the day came from the exchange's computerized quotation system which collapsed under the strain. Nowadays when any STOCK MARKET updates its antique rules, it is referred to as a Big Bang.

Big board

The popular name for the New York Stock Exchange (NYSE), the world's biggest STOCK MARKET in terms of the average daily value of the SHARES traded on it. The Big Board was once, literally, a big board on which the prices of shares were posted for all the traders milling around on the stock exchange floor to see. In today's COMPUTER age, however, little screens have taken over from big boards.

The NYSE is on Wall Street, the thoroughfare at the southern end of Manhattan that has become synonymous with twentieth-century capitalism.

Big eight

See ACCOUNTING FIRMS

Big four

The four large U.K. "clearing" banks—Barclays, Lloyds, Midland, and National Westminster—that dominate commercial banking in the United Kingdom. In many other countries commercial banking is similarly dominated by a Big Four or a Big Three.

The Boston Consulting Group has turned this observation into a wider, general rule (known as "The Rule of Three and Four"). It states that in a stable competitive MARKET there are never more than three significant competitors, the largest of which has no more than four times the MARKET SHARE of the smallest. Of course, the most treacherous MONOPOLY never has more than three significant competitors either.

Bill of exchange

Confirmation of a debt between two companies that is due to be paid at a future date, usually in 30, 60, or 90 days. The maturity varies according to common commercial practice in different countries. Bills of exchange have been popular since the fifteenth century. They were introduced by Italian traders and copied by their Flemish counterparts. They have developed into negotiable instruments that can be "accepted" (see ACCEPTANCE CREDIT) by a bank and then turned into ready cash. This separation of the money underlying a commercial transaction from the transaction itself is seen as a major step in the development of capitalism.

BILL OF LADING

The document given by a shipping or trucking COMPANY to the person whose goods it is transporting. The bill of lading acknowledges the amount of freight received, the condition it is in, and the terms under which it is being transported.

If the shipping company receives the freight in good condition, it gives a clean bill (as in "a clean bill of health"). If, however, it inserts a clause saying that the freight was not received as it should be, then the bill is known as a "dirty" bill of lading.

For the person whose goods are being shipped, the bill of lading is documentary proof of ownership. As such it can be used as security, for example, to DISCOUNT a bill of exchange received from the purchaser of the goods.

There are many different types of bills, most of them relating to the form of transport of the goods—for example, inland waterways bill, railway bill, liner bill, and so on.

BINARY SYSTEM

For no more special reason than the fact that we have ten fingers, our mathematics is based on the decimal system, that is, on the number ten. Hence the number 2,451 is actually $2 \times 10^3 + 4 \times 10^2 + 5 \times 10^1 + 1 \times 10^0$.

We could base our mathematics on any number, the number

two, for instance. In such a system, instead of needing ten digits (0 through 9) we need only two (1 and 0). The number 10,010 then becomes equal to $1 \times 2^4 + 0 \times 2^3 + 0 \times 2^2 + 1 \times 2^1 + 0 \times 2^0$. In the decimal system that is $16 + 2$, or 18.

A system based on two digits is called a binary system. It becomes particularly useful in electronics and COMPUTERS where switches are either on or off, and currents either flow or they do not flow. An "off" switch can represent 0 and an "on" switch 1. Rows and rows of switches can then be used to do all sorts of computations. (Note that mathematical operations are carried out in the binary system in the same way as in the decimal system. So $10,010 + 11,101 = 101,111$; or $18 + 29 = 47$.)

Biotechnology

A technology based on the use of living organisms to produce chemical changes and new materials. Biotechnology was believed (at the beginning of the 1980s) to hold great promise for the production of new products and of new ways to make old products (like insulin and antibiotics).

One branch, called genetic engineering, produced changes by reorganizing the genetic structure of different life forms. Not surprisingly it raised fears that communities might be in danger from the accidental escape of mutant life forms. So far such fears have been unfounded, except in the imaginations of Hollywood scriptwriters.

Despite attracting much venture CAPITAL, the biotechnology industry has yet to fulfill its promise.

Blue-chip

In casinos the most valuable chips used to be colored blue. Stock exchanges, which in many respects resemble casinos, adopted the expression "blue-chip" for their most valued investments.

These included both government securities and the SHARES of big, well-established companies considered to be the soundest industrial investments that the STOCK MARKET can provide.

BLUE-COLLAR WORKER

A reference to the blue uniforms that were once customary for workers to wear on the factory floor. This is in contrast to WHITE-COLLAR WORKER and is yet another example of the use of color in business language, along with blue-chip, gilt-edged, red tape, in the red, BROWN GOODS, and WHITE GOODS.

BOARD

The committee of directors officially appointed by the shareholders of a COMPANY to look after their interests. Many boards are called upon to do little more than meet once a month in the boardroom—a hallowed place that at other times remains uselessly empty—and then to enjoy a good lunch.

Keeping the board minutes (the record of the meeting) is one of the most important parts of the ritual of these monthly gatherings. Many boards are self-perpetuating oligarchies, selecting new directors from among their own close acquaintances. Shareholders have the right to reject the board's recommendations, but they rarely exercise that right. By and large, shareholders get the boards that they deserve.

Countries like Germany and Sweden have two-tier boards: a MANAGEMENT board made up of executive directors who "direct" the company's day-to-day business, and a supervisory board made up of nonexecutives who "supervise" the management board. The most striking difference between this board structure and the Anglo-Saxon structure is not so much its duality as the fact that company workers or their representatives sit on management boards.

What goes on in the boardroom is a travesty. The chairman doesn't want someone under him who is a threat, so he picks someone a little less capable. It's like an anti-Darwinian theory—the survival of the unfittest—and it's getting worse.

Carl Icahn, corporate raider, 1985

BOND

In its widest sense, any document that acknowledges the existence of a debt. In financial markets a bond is a fixed-interest security maturing in a stated time and issued by a government or corporation. Many such bonds are traded on the STOCK MARKET. They can change hands many times before they mature and are "redeemed" at their "face VALUE."

Bonds come in many shapes and sizes (see also BEARER BOND).

Convertible bond. A bond that may be exchanged for shares (or some other sort of security) after a certain amount of time and at the bondholder's discretion.

Indexed bond. A bond whose interest payments and CAPITAL value are adjusted according to the rate of INFLATION.

Irredeemable bond. Sometimes known as an "annuity" bond or "perpetual" bond, a bond that has no maturity date and on which interest is payable ad infinitum. It comes close to being the same as EQUITY.

Junk bond. A bond that is a load of rubbish or (more technically) a bond issued by a corporation that has less than a given CREDIT RATING from the major credit-rating agencies (Moody's and Standard & Poor's).

Performance bond. A pledge given by contractors that they will pay a certain sum of money should they fail to perform according to their CONTRACT.

Redeemable bond. A bond that may be repaid by the issuer when he or she wishes, after giving a certain amount of notice.

Savings bond. A savings instrument issued by governments to encourage small savers. It usually comes with tax advantages attached.

BONDED WAREHOUSE

A guarded warehouse in which importers can store goods duty free. The importers withdraw their goods (and pay duty on them) as and when they need them.

Bonded warehouses are often run by governments. When owned by a private firm, that firm gives the government a "bond" (or pledge) that it will faithfully carry out its duty (of ensuring that duty is paid on the goods).

BONUS

An extra payment made to employees or agents over and above what they can contractually expect.

BOOKKEEPING

The art of keeping a COMPANY'S books, that is, recording the day-to-day transactions of the company in financial terms. These books form the basis of the company's annual accounts. (See also DOUBLE-ENTRY)

BOSTON MATRIX

A concept invented by a firm of consultants (The Boston Consulting Group) in the 1960s. It provides a framework for thinking about different companies within a large group by defining them along two axes: their **MARKET SHARE** and the growth rate of the sector they are in.

The consultants divided the framework into four sections— **CASH COWS, DOGS, STARS,** and **QUESTION MARKS**—each requiring a different sort of strategic treatment. This proved to be an inspired way to give them a popular appeal, which has persisted ever since.

BOUTIQUE

A business with the characteristics of a boutique shop: it is small, it sells only the highest-quality merchandise, and it is located in a rather select part of town.

Boutiques are most often found in service industries, when highly respected professionals leave prestigious firms in order to start out on their own. A brand manager from Nestlé cannot easily leave the Swiss giant in order to set up his or her own chocolate business, but a consultant from McKinsey or a banker from Merrill Lynch can easily open her own boutique. All that is needed is a new secretary, a new telephone number, a new address, and some old clients.

BOYCOTT

An organized attempt to trade with a particular person, **COMPANY**, or country. Boycotts are notoriously difficult to enforce. **TRADE UNIONS** and pressure groups have occasionally tried to boycott companies whose policies they disapprove of, but such companies nearly always find somebody who is willing to do business with them, at a price.

Country boycotts are similarly difficult to enforce. The boycott of Rhodesia—before it became Zimbabwe—is a classic case. Rhodesia was able to get almost all it needed through neighboring South Africa.

*If this business were to be split up, I would be glad
to take the brands, trademarks and goodwill. You
could have all the bricks and mortar, and I would
fare better than you.*

John Stuart, when chairman of the Quaker food group

BRANDING

The attribution to a product of a name or TRADEMARK, which,
in the extreme, becomes almost synonymous with the product,
as Coke is to cola.

Companies with a strong brand have a valuable asset. An
IBM COMPUTER can be sold for more than an identical computer
without the famous three-letter acronym. Some companies try
to put a VALUE in their BALANCE SHEET on the premium that
they are able to charge because of their brand names.

The value of brand names in CONSUMER goods is being eroded
by retailers' "own label" products.

BRAND MANAGEMENT

The systematic development of a particular brand and its value.
There was a time when a brand manager was little more than
a liaison officer between a manufacturing COMPANY and its advertising agency. With the increasing value attributed to brands
in the 1980s (a value that is sometimes included in the BALANCE
SHEET), brand MANAGEMENT became upgraded. Brand managers
were seen as custodians of considerable value. Their job was to
nurture that value by promoting their brand successfully.

BREAK-UP VALUE

The value of a business were it to be broken up: the sum of the
prices fetched for all its ASSETS sold separately. This is very

different from the value of the assets sold together as a GOING CONCERN. In recent decades many businesses were taken over by people called "asset strippers" who had made the simple calculation that the value of the parts of a business were worth more than the whole. Once in control of the whole, they made big profits by selling off the pieces.

The break-up value of an individual asset (a car, say) is the value of all its bits and pieces (the plastic, electronics, scrap metal, and so on) sold separately.

BROKER

An intermediary who is employed by a COMPANY or person to trade on their behalf, usually in return for a fee or a percentage commission.

Brokers do not own the goods that they buy and sell, unlike "dealers" who actually buy goods before selling them to somebody else. Brokers come in at least 57 varieties.

Commodity brokers. Agents for buyers and sellers in different commodity MARKETS, either the metal markets, or the markets for "soft commodities" like coffee, cotton, and wheat.

Insurance brokers. Advisers to clients on the best companies for particular insurance CONTRACTS. Although they are not employed by insurance companies, the broker's income is derived from commissions from the insurer.

Pawnbrokers. People who lend money on the security of personal property that is deposited with them. The property can be retrieved once the loan and interest have been repaid in full within an agreed time limit.

Shipbrokers. Go-betweens for shipowners and for those who want cargo (or passengers) shipped.

Stockbrokers. People who buy stocks and SHARES on behalf of clients. On many stock exchanges stockbrokers used to be strictly separated from dealers in stocks and shares. That distinction has been eliminated recently in many markets.

He's called a broker because after dealing with him you are.

Aphorism

BROWN GOODS

An expression beloved by **MARKETING** people and **ADVERTISING** agencies. It refers to electrical goods that were traditionally sold to consumers in brown casings, such as radios, televisions, stereos, and so on. Now, of course, they are mostly sold in black casings, but they are still brown goods. (See also **WHITE GOODS**)

BUDGET

A forecast of revenue and expenditure for a forthcoming period for a part of a business. The process of drawing up budgets is something that every line manager quickly becomes familiar with—and just as quickly becomes disillusioned with. Budgets tend to be treated either with something bordering on the sanctity of a bank loan agreement or with the respect accorded to an insurance salesman. They are helpful only if linked to the **COMPANY'S** overall **STRATEGY** and goals, and only if they are flexible enough to account for intervening changes. (See **ZERO-BASE BUDGETING**)

A budget is a numerical check of your worst suspicions.

Anon

BUFFER INVENTORY

In general, an inventory of materials held in reserve at every stage of a production process, spares kept just in case there are delays in the supply of materials. It is expensive to sit on a permanent buffer inventory just in case of a rainy day, so modern inventory-CONTROL methods aim to cut buffer inventories down to a minimum. Such methods aim to supplant "just-in-case" with "JUST-IN-TIME."

More specifically, buffer inventories are inventories held in reserve by the managers of international commodity agreements. Countries that depend heavily on a single commodity for their export earnings (such as Zambia with its copper) get together and agree to maintain supplies of the commodity in order to stabilize its price.

Exporters argue that this is in the best interests of their customers, but commodity buffer inventories have almost invariably created difficulties. In 1986 the International Tin Agreement (ITA) fell apart when the manager of the buffer inventory bought so much tin that he ran out of money. The major tin-producing countries (like Malaysia) then refused to give him any more.

Bureaucracy defends the status quo after the quo has lost its status.

BUSINESS CYCLE

Businesses and national economies do not grow steadily in a straight line forever (although observers of the 1980s might be forgiven for having believed briefly that they do). Like the rest of us, business and trade go in cycles. They rise to a peak of activity before falling back into a recessionary sleep. They then wake up to begin the cycle all over again.

This is a finding based on past experience, but there is nothing to guarantee that it will continue to happen. Since World War II the cycles' periodicity in the Western world has been about 5 years. But in the 1980s almost 10 years passed between the trough of 1981 and the next major trough of 1990–1991.

People have attempted to link the business cycle to things

like the weather, or the effect of sunspots on harvests. A Russian economist, Nikolai Kondratieff, identified much longer cycles of some 50 to 60 years on which shorter cycles were superimposed. Kondratieff published his findings in the 1920s—before the Great Depression of the early 1930s—almost exactly 60 years ago.

The majority of businessmen are incapable of original thought because they are unable to escape from the tyranny of reason.

David Ogilvy

BUSINESS ETHICS

The body of principles and behavior that are morally acceptable for business. A series of corporate scandals in the 1980s brought business ethics out of the closet. Immoral (and illegal) behavior put the likes of Ivan Boesky and Michael Milken in prison.

Not all legal behavior is ethical, however. What about the advertisement that showed a specially reinforced Volvo not being crushed by a monster truck, while weakened rivals were? That was unethical, but nobody was charged with a crime. And what about Wellcome's pricing policy for its drug AZT when it was the only drug on the market offering any real hope to AIDS patients? To what extent should a company compromise its shareholders' interests in order to take the high moral ground?

Salomon Brothers, the SECURITIES firm that was badly affected in 1991 by a scandal involving its rigging of the U.S. government BOND MARKET, subsequently published a two-page advertisement in which its (new) chairman described a test that the COMPANY has devised to guide its employees:

Contemplating any business act, an employee should ask himself whether he would be willing to see it immediately described by an informed and critical reporter on the front page of his local paper, there to be read by his spouse, children and friends. At Salomon we simply want no part of any activities that pass legal tests but that we, as citizens, would find offensive.

BUSINESS PLAN

A necessary first step in starting a new business or business project, be it within an existing organization or as a new COMPANY starting from scratch. Without a business plan, no budding ENTREPRENEUR or ambitious executive will get through a bank manager's door or into a finance director's office.

Typically, a business plan will contain a one-year detailed projection of activity and a broader projection for the next three to five years. The plan will need to contain the following details:

- the business's goals
- how the operation is to be financed
- production of the goods or SERVICES to be sold, including details of premises and staff
- how the goods or services are to be marketed
- the general ENVIRONMENT in which the business will operate, its competitors, and possible future social and political change that might affect it.

BUSINESS SYSTEM

A way of looking at a business as a sequence of activities, each of which can be costed and analyzed on the basis of identical activities in the business's rivals. The system was developed and widely used by McKinsey's, a firm of MANAGEMENT consultants, and it provided the basis for Professor Michael Porter's theory about the VALUE CHAIN.

BY-PRODUCT

Something sellable that is produced as an incidental side effect of the manufacture of a main product—sawdust from a carpen-

ter, for example. In one sense the whole of the natural gas industry is only a by-product of the oil business.

By-products used to be considered rather inferior things; in
the verbal wars between butter and margarine, butter lovers
would maintain that margarine was a mere by-product from the
manufacture of soap powder. By-products have recently been
changing their image. Industry is increasingly looking to them
to help recycle waste produced by its main manufacturing
processes.

BYTE

A unit for measuring the storage capacity of a COMPUTER. One
byte equals eight bits, and a bit is a single binary digit (see
BINARY SYSTEM). Even portable computers nowadays have a storage capacity of several million bytes.

CAPACITY

The amount that a FACTORY or plant can produce in a given time. Most factories are working "below full capacity," if only because there are always some workers absent and machines in need of repair. When order books are empty, the "surplus capacity" of the factory rises. The ratio of surplus capacity to full capacity is a closely watched figure.

CAPITAL

Capital is dead labor that, vampire-like, lives only by sucking living labor, and lives the more, the more labor it sucks.
Karl Marx, *Das Kapital*

Capital is that part of the wealth of a country which is employed in production and consists of food, clothing, tools, raw materials, etc. necessary to give effect to labor.
David Ricardo

As these quotations from two great economists demonstrate, capital looks different from different angles. From one angle it is one of the three factors of production (along with LABOR and land). On the other hand, managers talk of human capital, the people who work in their business, and investors talk of share capital, the amount of money put into a COMPANY to buy its SHARES.

If only Groucho had written Das Kapital.
Graffiti

CAPITAL INTENSIVE

The description of industries that need a lot of CAPITAL to start them up and to keep them going. Such industries include those requiring sophisticated digging in the ground (such as the oil industry) or considerable infrastructure (such as railways). The high capital requirement acts as a barrier to entry into the industry; not everyone can open an oil refinery tomorrow.

Some businesses require very little capital (for example, service industries like ADVERTISING and accounting). They are referred to as LABOR-intensive and are being continually revived by people breaking away from old firms to start new ones. Who last started a steel business?

CAPITAL MARKETS

These are MARKETS for the long-term funds needed for CAPITAL investment, either to expand existing business projects or to start new ones. Capital markets can be divided into two.

Primary markets. In which new money is actually raised from investors in the form of SHARES, BONDS, or long-term bank loans. Companies in different countries raise long-term capital from these sources in varying proportions. German and Japanese companies are more dependent on bank loans; U.K. and U.S. companies more on shares.

Secondary markets. In which investors trade their shares or bonds and sell them to somebody else. Only bank loans cannot in general be traded, but even then there are exceptions. In the 1980s there was a thriving secondary market in long-term loans to developing countries.

This is a very clever system. It gives those raising the capital the security of knowing that they have funds for a long period. Yet it allows investors to get out of their investment immediately, if they so wish, by selling on the secondary market. Nevertheless there is a continuing conflict between the "short termism" that this encourages among investors and the "long termism" that is the real need of industry.

Capitalism without bankruptcy is like Christianity without hell.

Frank Borman, then CEO of Eastern Airlines

CARTEL

The formal organization of a group of manufacturers with the express purpose of reducing **COMPETITION** between them by, for example, fixing prices. The most famous cartel is the **ORGANIZATION OF PETROLEUM EXPORTING COUNTRIES** (OPEC). Cartels attempt to give themselves the economic benefits of a **MONOPOLY**, but when push comes to shove they are only as strong as their weakest member.

Cartels are like babies; we tend to be against them until we have one of our own.

Anon

CASE-STUDY METHOD

A method of studying business that relies on the use of "cases," that is, written examples of actual companies and particular problems that they have faced. Students discuss the cases, usually in small teams, in order to come up with recommended courses of action that they can then present to the whole class.

The method has been criticized on several grounds.

• It is unreal. By and large, real business problems need to be solved in "real time" and in a hurry, not in a leisurely academic atmosphere.

- It can make business seem like more than a series of problems looking for solutions.
- Cases are limited to those that the teaching staff have been able to put together. In many schools that has made them too parochial. Students want more international material.

To help get around the last problem, a number of "clearing houses" for case studies have been set up. These enable business schools to purchase each other's material. To improve the quality of cases, there are a number of competitions giving prizes for Case Study of the Year.

CASH COWS

One of the four elements of the BOSTON MATRIX, the most famous corporate concept ever invented. Cash cows are companies that fall into the bottom right-hand quadrant of a diagram whose vertical axis measures growth of the sector and whose horizontal axis measures relative MARKET SHARE.

So cash cows are companies with a high market share in sectors with low growth, like Kellogg's breakfast cereals or Marlboro in the cigarette market.

CASH FLOW

A statement of the amount of cash flowing into a COMPANY during a specified period. This can be calculated from the accountants' concept of net PROFIT. Subtract the amount paid in DIVIDENDS from the net profit, and then add back noncash expenses that have been subtracted, such as DEPRECIATION. Finally, subtract noncash revenues like deferred income, and there you have it.

Cash flow is an important indicator of a company's ability to pay future dividends and of its ability to finance future investment from its own resources. It is a cheaper source of funds than expensive bank loans or rights issues.

Some companies (like General Electric and the big Japanese

car and electronics firms) have enormous cash flows that they are unable to invest. That leaves them looking rather like banks, holding huge deposits of other people's (that is, their shareholders') money. Strange that they never think of giving it back to the shareholders for them to invest.

Ways to improve cash flow include the following:

- Make special bank arrangements to speed up transfers of funds between accounts.
- Offer cash discounts for early payment.
- Send invoices out more quickly.
- Use telephone reminders.
- Demand cash on delivery.
- Minimize cash tied up elsewhere (in loans to staff, for instance).

CASH ON DELIVERY

Cash on delivery (COD) indicates that a transaction requires cash (or an equivalent) to be paid for goods at the place and time that they are delivered to the purchaser.

CATCH-22

The title of a novel by Joseph Heller has become a catchphrase for situations that can also be described as "Heads I win, tails you lose." Commonly found where there are restrictive employment practices—for example, people cannot work as journalists until they are members of the journalists' union, but to join the union they have to have worked as journalists.

CENTRALIZATION

The process of concentrating CONTROL of an organization at its center. The opposite of delegation. Centralization is currently unfashionable as a MANAGEMENT style, but it is frequently found in companies that are driven largely by the efforts of one person.

It may be a mistake to consider centralization and decentralization as mutually exclusive. Tight centralized control of **BUDGETING** leads to decentralized control of the methods of achieving the budget's targets.

Responsibility is the great developer of men.

Mary Parker Follett

CHAIR

The person in charge of the meetings of a **COMPANY'S BOARD**. The chair also has the casting vote should the directors of the board be evenly split on a decision.

Many company chairs are also the company's chief executive, a combination of duties that is increasingly being questioned. The chair of the board is theoretically the leading representative of the company's shareholders; the chief executive is the leading representative of the managers and other employees. It is a lot to expect one person to play both roles in the best interests of both groups.

CHANGE

Change has become a prime preoccupation of managers, and rightly so. Few companies carry on for long anywhere in the world without undergoing internal restructuring, merger, divestiture, or significant redundancies, and, externally, companies' markets are changing faster than ever.

Awareness of the permanence of change is not new: what may be new is an awareness that change is not even a process of evolution toward permanence. Companies are simply wasting their time if they are looking for a fixed state in which all need for further change ceases.

Change is uncomfortable and strongly resisted. The Conference Board, a Washington-based **MANAGEMENT** research organization, has found 10 particularly common reasons why it is resisted.

1. The purpose of the change is not made clear.
2. The details of the change are poorly communicated.
3. The people affected are not involved in the planning of the change.
4. The change is introduced too quickly or too slowly.
5. Key job characteristics are changed.
6. Key people are not seen as being completely behind the change.
7. There is the fear of failure.
8. The status quo cannot be re-established if the change proves to be a failure.
9. The people affected believe it reflects badly on their past performance.
10. There is a lack of confidence in people's capacity to implement the change.

I have come to the conclusion that the decisive change which underlies the rise of organizations is the shift from viewing the worker as a cost center to viewing him as a resource.

Peter Drucker

CHAPTER 11

Part of the 1978 Bankruptcy Act, providing a novel approach to troubled companies. Before Chapter 11 was written, a faltering **COMPANY'S CREDITORS** either got everything back because the company got itself out of trouble, or they got virtually nothing because the company collapsed. It was an all-or-nothing affair, with no options in between.

Chapter 11 provided options by allowing the DEBTOR company and its creditors to work together to find a solution. For example, the creditors might agree to take, say, 40% of what they were owed and write off the rest.

The process was criticized following cases like that of Manville Corporation, an asbestos company that sought the protection of Chapter 11 because it said that its liability for asbestos-induced diseases among its employees could force it into LIQUIDATION.

Is Chapter 11 what comes after following the ten commandments?

Anon

Charge

This is not just what an aggressive COMPANY does when entering a new MARKET nor the price of a service (note that lawyers and accountants have charges; grocers and booksellers have prices), but a charge (or lien) is also a form of security taken by a lender over property that has been purchased by the borrower (often a home purchased with a mortgage). Such a charge has to be registered with an official body. If the borrower fails to meet the conditions of the loan agreement, the lender can take possession of the property over which it has the charge. (See also FLOATING CHARGE)

CIF

See COST, INSURANCE, FREIGHT

CLOSED SHOP

The situation where LABOR unions have compelled managers to agree that nobody who is not a member of their union may be employed in a particular business or FACTORY. Though more discreet, the professional associations of accountants, lawyers, and doctors frequently have much the same effect as the closed shop of the BLUE-COLLAR WORKER.

COD

See CASH ON DELIVERY

COGNITIVE DISSONANCE

A psychological theory that has been widely used to underpin certain types of ADVERTISING and MARKETING. The theory of cognitive dissonance says that when people's beliefs conflict with their behavior it creates "dissonance." That compels them either to change their beliefs to suit their behavior or to change their behavior to suit their beliefs.

Thus, what do manufacturers who are all in favor of free trade do when their domestic MARKET is decimated by cheap imports? Either they decide they are no longer in favor of free trade, or they start to manufacture something else.

Advertisers attempt to create dissonance in CONSUMERS' minds by suggesting that there is a better product than the one they are using for the job they want it to do. To resolve the dissonance, consumers then have to either disbelieve the advertisement or buy the other product.

COLLATERAL

Something that a borrower provides (over and above a trustworthy smile) as security for a loan. If the lender does not get the loan back, it can take the collateral instead. Collateral is commonly held in the form of a CHARGE over property, but it can be in the form of BEARER BONDS or other sorts of title to property held by the lender until it is repaid in full.

COLLECTIVE BARGAINING

The process of negotiating wage and salary increases collectively rather than individually. This involves (sometimes lengthy) negotiations between TRADE UNIONS and employers. Most PUBLIC-SECTOR employees' pay is determined by collective bargaining. In the PRIVATE SECTOR, on the other hand, most managers' salaries are determined by individual NEGOTIATION.

COMMERCIAL BANK

The most visible type of bank to the general public, one that provides deposit-taking services and loans, and that is usually involved in its country's check-clearing system. Commercial banks are the ones with branches on every main street in the land.

They are commercial in two senses: they provide short-term loans and other services to industry and commerce (once upon a time purely for the financing of trade), and they are commercial organizations themselves, intent upon making a profit.

Although in many countries long-established distinctions between different types of banks are being eroded (many commercial banks, for example, are now also investment banks), it is still worth defining them.

Central bank. The official organization at the heart of a country's monetary system. Central banks carry out any combination of four different functions. They act as banker to both the government and to the commercial banks, they print the nation's notes and mint its coins, and they supervise the banking system.

Investment bank. A term originating in the United States for banks that specialize in the provision of long-term loans and in the raising of equity for industry. The Glass-Steagall Act of 1933 strictly separates investment banks (which can raise

CAPITAL for companies) from commercial banks (which cannot), but even that separation is becoming blurred with the years.

MERCHANT BANK. A term for old, established British banks that advise and help companies raise capital and take over each other. Many of them still carry the names of the families that founded them centuries ago (as the financial arms of big "merchant" trading houses). They include families like the Barings, Hambros, Rothschilds, and Schroders.

Savings bank and building society. Popular in many European countries, such an institution traditionally collects the money of small savers and passes it on to others to lend. Money-transmission services, such as checks, are not always provided.

Universal bank. The sort of bank, common in Europe, that can do almost anything it wants because neither tradition (as in the United Kingdom) nor legislation (as in the United States) has separated investment banking from commercial banking. Germany's Deutsche Bank, for example, is able to satisfy Daimler-Benz's short-term trade financing requirements; to raise capital by underwriting a new equity issue for Daimler-Benz; to hold Daimler-Benz shares itself; and to provide Daimler-Benz with a chairman from among its own top managers. It is indeed universal.

> *Good bankers, like good tea, can only be appreciated when they are in hot water.*
>
> Jaffar Hussein, governor of the Malaysian central bank

COMMERCIAL PAPER

A short-term debt instrument, commercial paper has a maturity of 2 to 270 days, although the most popular maturities are within 30 to 90 days. Commercial paper does not usually pay interest. Rather, it is sold at a DISCOUNT, with the full amount repayable on maturity.

Commercial paper is issued by big, well-known industrial and financial corporations and, by and large, is also bought by big, well-known industrial and financial corporations. It is not designed for small private investors, since it is usually issued in minimum dollops of $100,000.

A committee is an animal with four back legs.

John Le Carré

COMMODITY AGREEMENTS

Agreements between nations that produce and consume commodities. They agree that they will use various techniques to stabilize the price of things like tin, rubber, coffee, and cocoa. The techniques include the building up of buffer stocks to be drawn upon when the MARKET is in short SUPPLY, or the application of quotas to restrict supply when there is a surplus.

Stable prices give CONSUMERS and producers certainty about (respectively) their COSTS and revenues, so in principle everybody is in favor of commodity agreements. In practice they have proved remarkably difficult to manage. Nations have always been tempted to slip out of them when they are inconvenient. In 1986 the tin agreement—one of the more successful at stabilizing prices—fell apart because signatory governments refused to give the buffer stock manager more money to buy more tin.

COMPANY

A legal entity formed by a group of individuals for the purpose of doing business. The company is recognized in law as a separate entity having rights and duties distinct from those of the individuals who form it. They can all die, yet the company continues to exist.

The most significant right for most companies is that of **LIMITED LIABILITY**. The duties that go with that right are numerous and laid down in company law. They include restrictions on what directors can do and requirements to register information so that it is accessible to the general public.

The great modern corporations are so similar to independent or semi-independent states of the past that they can only be fully understood in terms of political and constitutional history, and management can only be properly studied as a branch of government.

Anthony Jay

COMPARATIVE ADVANTAGE

An economic idea first propounded by the economist David Ricardo in the early nineteenth century, when arguments in favor of free trade were not taken so much for granted as they are today.

The principle of comparative advantage says that the world will be better off if each country concentrates on producing what it does best, even if what it does second-best is better than what another country does best. Production will be maximized if each concentrates on what it is best suited to produce and then all trade their goods among themselves.

COMPATIBLE

What bits and pieces of **COMPUTERS** are when they can be linked up and worked together. For instance, a printer is IBM compatible when it can print material from an IBM PC.

COMPETITION

The eternal contest between business firms to see which can perform the best either in terms of MARKET share, PROFIT, or some other recognized yardstick. Competition is rarely pure and unqualified.

Cut-throat competition. A blood-curdling concept that goes back to the military origins of MANAGEMENT. It usually refers to situations where supply exceeds demand, and suppliers cut prices to maintain their share of a market, well aware that some of their competitors must collapse.

Healthy competition. Competition between firms that are not believed to be indulging in unfair practices.

Monopolistic competition. Sounds like a contradiction in terms, for is not MONOPOLY the absence of competition? But this is an economists' expression, and for them it means something between a total monopoly and perfect competition (see below), that is, virtually all of business life.

Perfect competition. The theoretical economists' Valhalla where a large number of buyers and sellers of a homogeneous product ensure that no one of them can affect its price. Firms maximize their profits by producing just enough goods to make their marginal COST equal to their marginal revenue.

Unfair competition. Where manufacturers make dishonest claims about a product, for example. Much competition that is described as unfair is not.

Competition brings out the best in products and the worst in people.

David Sarnoff, former president of RCA

COMPETITIVENESS

The ability of a country or business to produce goods and SER-VICES that can compete successfully in world MARKETS. Two international organizations based in Switzerland (the World Economic Forum and IMD) produce an annual ranking of world competitiveness based on a combination of factual data (such as relative labor costs) and the subjective opinions of a large sample of top businesspeople (on subjects such as the efficiency of a country's distribution system).

In 1992 the top 10 countries in the rankings were as follows:

1. Japan
2. Germany
3. Switzerland
4. Denmark
5. United States
6. Netherlands
7. Austria
8. Sweden
9. Ireland
10. Finland

COMPUTER

The computer has been to the twentieth century what the steam engine was to the nineteenth. Yet nobody has won a Nobel prize for its invention. It has crept, not leapt, into our lives.

The computer is a machine that harnesses the physics of electronics, the chemistry of silicon, and the mathematics of the BINARY SYSTEM. It uses them to store information, to process it, and then to perform an infinitely large number of tasks with a speed and efficiency that, without the benefit of hindsight, we might have assumed would by now have made us all redundant.

In fact the opposite has occurred. In industries like banking and accounting, where the computer has obvious potential to reduce employment, the workforce has increased dramatically since its invention. In industry and commerce, computers are used in all sorts of ways: as calculators in the accounts department, as robots in the production department, and as typewriters in head offices.

There are all sorts of them.

LAPTOP computers

Mainframe computers. The old-fashioned giants that used to sit in the COMPANY'S basement and were sometimes rented out at weekends.

Minicomputers. Smaller than a mainframe but with a central processor powerful enough to service a NETWORK.

Personal computers. Known as PCs, these are the sort of computers that sit comfortably on one person's desk and are sometimes light enough to be carried around.

Supercomputers. Extra powerful machines that use the latest computer technology to perform amazingly complex operations amazingly fast.

One computer manufacturer was so successful he had to move to smaller premises.

Anon

CONCENTRATION

There is a tendency for industrial sectors in developed economies to become increasingly dominated by a few large firms. Activity becomes "concentrated" in their hands. In the oil industry the concentration in the hands of the "Seven Sisters" is well known. In Europe it is evident in banking, where the business is heavily concentrated in the hands of three or four almost indistinguishable institutions in France, Germany, and the United Kingdom.

No COMPANY ever had the ambition to become smaller, so the trend toward concentration is built in. It is held in check to some extent by laws that prevent takeovers from giving one firm a "dominant share" of any particular MARKET.

Karl Marx thought that concentration would be the ruin of capitalism, creating a small elite and a vast exploited mass that would eventually rise up in revolt. He got the right cause, however, but the wrong effect. The concentration of power and resources in the hands of East European elites was the ruin of communism.

CONCESSION

A special right given to somebody, usually for a price, not always paid in cash. The following are some examples:

- the exclusive right to sell the products of a manufacturer within a certain area
- the right to dig for minerals on a particular plot of land
- a tax allowance given to encourage things like exports and investment in underdeveloped regions

CONGLOMERATE

A group that owns companies in a wide range of different businesses. For example, Daimler-Benz makes cars and bits and pieces of airplanes, and it runs naval yards. The advantage of conglomerates is supposed to be that they spread risk. Thus, for Daimler-Benz, if the defense market is in the doldrums, its earnings will be supported by CONSUMER expenditure on cars, and so on.

Conglomerates in manufacturing industries were very fashionable in the 1960s and 1970s, but by the end of the 1980s, many were being dismantled on the advice of management consultants who realized that a COMPANY that ran one business well could not necessarily do the same with any business. There was no evidence to suggest that conglomerates were more than the sum of their individual parts.

CONSIGNMENT

Goods consigned (sent) from one place to another. Goods sent "on consignment" to an AGENT by a manufacturer have been sent on a sale-or-return basis. Agents do not pay for them until they sell them, and any that they do not sell are returned to sender.

CONSOLIDATION

A method of treating a group—that is, a parent COMPANY and its subsidiaries—as a single unit for accounting purposes. In most developed countries consolidation is now a legal requirement for large companies.

Consolidation developed in the English-speaking business world to meet the demands of investors for a complete picture of the company that they owned. In extremis a parent company might exist only to hold the SHARES of its subsidiaries. Without consolidation its financial statements would be just a list of its shareholdings. Through consolidation shareholders would get an idea of the businesses the subsidiaries were actually in.

It is less popular in continental Europe where legal considerations are more influential than investors' fancy. A group does not actually exist as a legal entity; you cannot sue it. And the tax inspector does not assess it for tax; the taxable entity is each individual corporation. So why draw up accounts for it?

Consolidation is a rather complicated process that involves adding together ASSETS and LIABILITIES, and revenues and expenses, of the parent and its subsidiaries. Bits here and there are then subtracted to avoid double-counting transactions between companies within the group. The ways in which companies consolidate subsidiaries in different countries are very inconsistent, but then they are often inconsistent within the same country.

CONSORTIUM

The combination of a number of large companies for the purposes of one specific project. This is commonly done for very large building projects—like dams and bridges—that are too large for one COMPANY to undertake alone. Consortia are useful too when a number of specialist skills are needed for a job that cannot be found within a single firm. This was the logic behind consortium banks, popular in the 1970s and early 1980s. They brought together banks of different nationalities with specialist knowledge of different MARKETS. Unlike most consortia, though, they were not disbanded once their specific task was done.

CONSUMER

The ultimate beneficiary of industrialization, and the only reason for any business to exist. The role of the consumer has changed in recent years. For as long as industry could scarcely supply enough goods and SERVICES to meet "consumer demand," it could afford to be cavalier about consumers' attitudes. Most of its attention then was forced on placating LABOR and maximizing production.

That situation changed sometime in the 1960s. Since then consumers have become more discerning. They have more choices, and manufacturers have to woo them. Out of this grew (first) the consumer movement, led by pioneers like Ralph Nader. It set out to protect consumers themselves against commercial exploitation. It was followed by the green movement, which was also consumer driven out of a concern for the damage that industry was causing to the environment.

Over time, the power structure within corporations has

changed. Real power has shifted among the corporation's different constituencies: first it resided in the owner/manager, the original nineteenth-century capitalist. Then it switched to labor with the growth of TRADE UNIONS and the post-war LABOR shortages in the West. Then it was the turn of the shareholder briefly to be "king" as CAPITAL again became the key factor of production. Now, perhaps, it is the turn of the environmentalist as the guardian of finite resources, another factor of production.

The consumer is not a moron; she is your wife.

David Ogilvy

CONSUMER DURABLES

CONSUMER goods (that is, goods on sale to the general public) that are designed to last and to be used over a period of time, such as dishwashers and televisions. Because they are purchased infrequently, consumer durables have certain special properties.

- They are less sensitive to price than so-called fast-moving consumer goods (like toothpaste, chewing gum, and so forth). To some extent customers are prepared to wait until they can afford better quality.

- Manufacturers have to be looking continually for new MARKETS to maintain sales; fast-moving consumer goods can maintain sales by sticking to the same market.

- They are more susceptible to downturns in the BUSINESS CYCLE. It is easier to tighten your belt by making do with an old washing machine than by giving up steak.

CONSUMPTION FUNCTION

The relationship between consumption and income. In general, the more income people have the more they consume. The propensity to consume decreases, however, as income increases.

On occasions consumption can exceed income by drawing on past savings or borrowing against future income. But as Mr. Micawber said in Charles Dickens's *David Copperfield:*

Annual income twenty pounds, annual expenditure nineteen nineteen six, result happiness. Annual income twenty pounds, annual expenditure twenty pounds ought and six, result misery.

CONTINGENT LIABILITY

A liability that may arise if something else happens. An example would be a COMPANY that currently had a lawsuit against it claiming that it had polluted a large area of land. If found liable, the company could face a huge bill for the cost of repairing the damage. In its annual report to shareholders the company might want to mention that it has such a liability, contingent upon the outcome of the lawsuit.

CONTRACT

An agreement in which one party agrees to supply goods or SERVICES to another in return for a "consideration," usually money. The agreement can be verbal but in business it is usually written; even then there can be disagreement over what the agreement means. All contracts can be renegotiated or broken, and some are void from the start because they involve illegal acts such as murder or INDUSTRIAL ESPIONAGE. The remedy for breach is usually damages; only in a very few cases can the buyer insist on "specific performance."

CONTROL

A word that is used in several different business contexts.

- A COMPANY that holds more than 50% of the voting rights of another company is said to control that company.
- Stock (or INVENTORY) control is a system of checking a company's inventory to see that it contains all that the records say it should.

- **QUALITY CONTROL**
- Control systems are a combination of instruments used to check and operate automatically the controls of various production processes in industry. (See **ROBOTICS**)
- In **DIRECT MAIL**, a control sample is used as a yardstick against which the success of future mail shots can be judged.

COPYRIGHT

The legal right of the creator of a literary, musical, or artistic work to reproduce that work for gain, and to prevent anybody else from doing so. In many countries of the world copyright protection is weak; witness the plethora of pirated music and videocassettes that can be bought very cheaply in parts of the Far East.

The latest round of talks under the GATT is set upon tightening copyright protection in these places. Such protection will greatly benefit the United States and Europe at the expense of countries whose individually creative work nobody else finds particularly interesting.

CORE COMPETENCE

When industrial conglomerates became outmoded in the 1980s, the fashion was for companies to return to their core competence, the business that they were particularly good at. **MANAGEMENT** consultants and writers like Tom Peters and Robert Waterman enthusiastically encouraged conglomerates to divest themselves of everything else.

CORPORATE CULTURE

Some still deny that this has any significance for a corporation. One American manager claimed that the only culture in his organization was in the yogurt sold in the cafeteria. However, the influence of men like Tom Peters and Robert Waterman has convinced most managers that culture (that is, an organization's distinctive pattern of ideas and behavior) does matter. In their book *In Search of Excellence,* Peters and Waterman found that "the dominance and coherence of culture proved to be an essential quality of excellent companies."

Japanese companies have very strong cultures enforced by group activities (like early morning singing sessions) and internal slogans (Sony's BMW—Beat Matsushita Whatever; Kao's KPG—Kill Procter & Gamble). In part, this flows from Japan's attitude to society and the role of the individual in it.

The fact that corporate cultures are strongly influenced by national and sectoral norms has led to widespread interest from multinationals in the foreign cultures in which they are working.

CORPORATE FINANCE

Considered the snazzy part of investment or MERCHANT BANK-ING, this helps companies decide what their financial needs are and then arranges to satisfy them. It is based on a close familiarity with the COMPANY'S CAPITAL structure and with merchant banks that owe each other favors.

CORPORATE GOVERNANCE

The manner in which corporations are governed, something that differs from country to country. In Anglo-Saxon economies the ultimate authority is given to shareholders, the owners of the corporation who take risks with their money.

Successful Anglo-Saxon corporate empire builders (like Lord Hanson) have grown by setting out to satisfy shareholders first and last. "The shareholder is king," said Hanson on more than one occasion. In such societies hostile takeovers occur as struggles between competing sets of shareholders. Other "constituencies" of the corporation—employees, suppliers, and CREDITORS—can but watch and wait.

In Germany and Japan corporate governance is rather different. Other constituencies (particularly employees and banks) have a greater say in their corporation's future (through workers' councils, representation on the board, or Japan's unique process of consensus forming). In these countries hostile takeovers are frowned upon and fiercely resisted. The Japanese wonder why one alien shareholder should have the right to put at risk a host of corporate relationships built up over many years. They believe in recognizing that all constituents take risks in their relationship with a corporation, not just shareholders.

The man who is denied the opportunity of taking decisions of importance begins to regard as important the decisions that he is allowed to take.

C. Northcote Parkinson

CORPORATE IDENTITY

This is a COMPANY'S signature, the name and logo by which it is immediately identified. The rash of mergers and corporate restructurings in the 1980s (and the mere passage of time) left many companies with an identity that no longer suited their business. This presented a fabulous opportunity for design firms to create new logos (and sometimes even new names) for more appropriate images.

The immediate COST of such an overhaul can run into tens of thousands of dollars. When its practical implications are considered, it can run into millions. In 1989 British Petroleum said that it expected to pay some £100 million over five years to implement its new green logo, printing it on all its service stations, hard hats, letterheads, offshore platforms, and so on.

A MULTINATIONAL COMPANY has to be very careful with the colors and symbols that it chooses; they can mean very different things in different places. Mitsubishi found its color scheme gave an impression of strength and vitality in Japan, but it looked cheap and nasty in Europe. Deutsche Bank's blue and white was fine in Germany but a problem in France where it looked too much like the local tricolor.

CORPORATION TAX

Tax imposed on the PROFITS of a COMPANY. All countries tax corporations in this way, but there are a number of differences in the details of how they do it.

The rates in different countries vary, and some have a specially low rate for small companies (or for companies that make small profits, which may not be the same thing). Countries also differ in the way in which they calculate the profits on which the tax is imposed. Adjustments have to be made to the company's profit as calculated by its accountants before arriving at its taxable profit. These mostly relate to accelerated rates of DEPRECIATION that governments allow in order to encourage capital investment.

The final difference lies in the treatment of DIVIDENDS. These are paid out of profits that have already been subjected to corporation tax. In the so-called classical system of taxation they are then taxed again in the hands of the recipient shareholder. This amounts to double taxation, an injustice that countries increasingly try to avoid. One way of doing so is by the imputation system of corporation tax. This imputes to the shareholder a tax credit for some or all of the tax already paid on the dividends by the company in the form of corporation tax.

One important consequence of pushing for the imputation system rather than the classical system is the effect it has on a company's capital structure. Companies have a natural preference for loan capital (the interest on which is fully deductible for tax purposes) over EQUITY (whose dividends are not deductible). That preference is magnified if dividends are taxed not once but twice, while interest payments are not taxed at all.

Cost

At its most basic, the amount of money that has to be paid in order to buy something. For example, "What is the cost of that doggy in the window?" From there accountants, economists, and MANAGEMENT experts have stretched the use of this little word a long way.

Average cost. The cost per unit of a business's output

Carrying cost. The cost of carrying (holding) stocks, machines, and factories. The carrying cost is the amount that the money used to buy and maintain these ASSETS could earn if it were sitting in a bank.

CURRENT COST

DIRECT COST

FIXED COST

HISTORIC COST

INDIRECT COST

Marginal cost. The cost of increasing a business's output by a single unit

OPPORTUNITY COST

Overhead cost (See OVERHEADS)

Production cost. The total cost of getting a product to the factory gate ready for distribution

REPLACEMENT COST

Transaction cost. The cost attached to carrying out a transaction, for example, a bank's commission for buying foreign exchange

Variable cost. Costs that vary in proportion to the quantity of goods produced, such as lighting, heating, and wages

Cost accounting

The detailed breaking down of the COSTS of manufacturing a product or of producing a service. Cost accounting soon runs up against the age-old problem of what to do about overheads, but it is invaluable in deciding on PRICING or in identifying where cost savings can be made.

COST-BENEFIT ANALYSIS

An essential element in all corporate planning: a systematic attempt to measure the VALUE of all the benefits that will accrue from a particular sort of expenditure. It attempts to answer the question "Is this particular investment going to be cost effective?"

There are three main elements to the task.

1. The identification of all the consequences of the expenditure. Nowadays that will have to include things like the harmless disposal of any waste that a new plant might produce.

2. An attempt to put a money value on all the costs and all the benefits. This is never easy. How do you measure the value of the improvement in staff morale from moving a plant out of the center of a grimy industrial town to a new GREENFIELD SITE?

3. The discounting of expected future costs and revenues in order to express them in current money values.

COST, INSURANCE, FREIGHT

Commonly known by its acronym CIF, the part of a trade CONTRACT that binds the exporter to pay not only the COST of getting the goods ready for transport, but also the cost of transporting them and of insuring them while in transit. (See FREE ON BOARD)

COST OF CAPITAL

Superficially a fairly easy calculation of the relative costs of different types of CAPITAL, such as loans, EQUITY, BONDS, and so on. The cost of equity is the DIVIDEND, and the cost of the rest is interest.

The first complication comes from taxation (see **CORPORA-TION TAX**), which puts the net cost of equity on a par with the gross cost of loans. Then there is the question of the degree of flexibility that corporations have in altering dividend payments. Cutting the dividend does not necessarily reduce the cost of capital. If the **COMPANY** is quoted, the stock market is sure to mark down the price of the company's **SHARES** as a consequence. And that presents an extra cost.

COTTAGE INDUSTRY

A business that could be run out of a cottage, like weaving, pottery, and clock making. But not all cottage industries are relics from before the **INDUSTRIAL REVOLUTION**. Modern **HIGH-TECH** businesses can also be cottage industries. In the Caribbean and on the west coast of Ireland, for example, there is a sizable cottage industry in processing **COMPUTER** data sent by satellite from the United States to these sources of cheap **LABOR**.

COUNTERTRADE

A form of international **BARTER** in which goods and **SERVICES** are traded between countries for other goods and services rather than for cash. Countertrading has been a particularly popular way of trading with cash-starved Eastern Europe in recent years.

Shortage of cash is not the only reason for countertrade deals. Members of OPEC have found countertrade deals a useful way of getting round OPEC-imposed production quotas.

Deals can become extremely complex: a multibillion-dollar deal between Turkey and the former Soviet Union, for instance, involved the export of huge quantities of Soviet natural gas to Turkey in return for a variety of Turkish products, ranging from fruit and textiles to engineering services. Such deals require someone (a bank or government department) to act as a sort of clearing/payment house. In the above example, the Turkish gas **CONSUMER** has to pay the Turkish engineering company; there is no way the engineer will accept payment in gas.

Anybody contemplating a countertrade deal would be well advised to get in touch with the specialist countertrade departments that now exist in many of the big international banks.

CREATIVE ACCOUNTING

A much-quoted story tells of an applicant for an accounting job who at his INTERVIEW was presented with a bundle of figures and asked to calculate the PROFIT. "Which profit did you have in mind?" he asked, and he immediately got the job.

There are few absolutes in accounting; much of its art lies in interpretation. And within any interpretation there is scope for "creative accounting," something that makes the picture look prettier than it would otherwise. In the 1980s no go-go COMPANY could afford to be without a creative accountant or two.

CREDIT GAP

The intellectual chasm between the interests of a seller in getting paid as quickly as possible and the interests of a buyer in paying as late as possible.

CREDIT NOTE

An acknowledgment by a seller of goods or SERVICES that the buyer has been overcharged. The note gives the buyer the right to purchase goods in the future up to a stated amount.

CREDITOR

A COMPANY or individual to whom money is owed by a DEBTOR. (See also PREFERENTIAL CREDITOR)

CREDIT RATING

An assessment of the creditworthiness of a COMPANY, an individual, or a debt instrument. Two large firms dominate the business: Moody's and Standard & Poor's.

Credit-rating agencies supply (for a fee) analyses of creditworthiness for two types of customer.

- Traders who are about to do business with somebody for the first time and who need to get a feel for how much credit they can extend to that person or company, and for how long.

- Investors who want to have an assessment of the quality of a particular corporate debt instrument that they are thinking of buying.

Credit rating has come a long way from its origins as a private arrangement between a seller and a potential customer's bank, entered into with the full knowledge of the potential customer. There is now a secondary MARKET in credit ratings, and they can be passed around without the subject of the rating knowing anything about it. This practice has been controlled by legislation, and anybody now has the right to see any information about themselves held by a credit-rating agency. They also have the right to have it corrected if it is incorrect.

CRISIS MANAGEMENT

Most managers' regular jobs are interrupted occasionally by a crisis. Since such an event is an extreme of one sort or another, its consequences can also be extreme. So the proper handling of crises is of vital importance to a business. The classic case of crisis MANAGEMENT occurred in 1990 when the Perrier bottled water company withdrew 160 million bottles from shops around the world after unacceptably high levels of benzene had been found in its water.

Learning about crisis management is a bit like learning the safety instructions in an aircraft before takeoff: you hope you will never need them, but you are not going to skip the class.

Here are a few widely recommended hints.

- Look out for advance warning of an impending crisis.

- Have a contingency plan and an alternate product or process ready.

- Speed of reaction is vital.

- Do not overreact.
- Watch out to see if competitors are trying to take advantage of your crisis.
- Be prepared to give up MARKET SHARE initially.
- Do not assume that everybody is hostile, and do not clam up.
- A crisis is the time to call upon goodwill that has been fostered during the good times.

CRITICAL PATH ANALYSIS

A way of planning how to undertake a complicated task—such as the building of a new factory or the removal of a large office to a new site—in as short a time as possible. Critical path analysis (CPA) depends on identifying the following factors:

- the operations that need to be taken to complete the task
- how the operations relate to each other
- how long each operation takes

These can then be represented graphically by a series of interlocking chains. The links that combine to require the longest time represent the "critical path." All other operations are then programmed to fit into this schedule.

CROSS-RATE

The EXCHANGE RATE between two currencies calculated via a third currency, usually the dollar. Suppose there are 90 chetrums (the currency of Bhutan) to the dollar, and 900 pa'anga (the currency of Tonga) to the dollar. The cross-rate for Bhutanese travelers to Tonga is then 10 pa'angas to the chetrum.

CURRENT ACCOUNT

A type of bank account from which money can be withdrawn immediately without the formal period of notice required by other forms of accounts. Also that part of a nation's trading account that shows the VALUE of its recent imports and exports of goods and SERVICES.

CURRENT ASSET

An ASSET that can be consumed by a business, now or in the near future. An example is RAW MATERIALS.

CURRENT COST

An accounting concept: the amount it would cost a COMPANY to buy one of its ASSETS today.

CUSTOMER LOYALTY

The faithfulness of customers to a particular product or manufacturer. In some industries customer loyalty is very valuable, but beware: it can sometimes be mistaken for inertia. CONSUMERS used to be loyal to their cars, buying the same manufacturer's models again and again.

DATABASE

A collection of information stored in a COMPUTER in an orderly way.

DATA PROCESSING

The placing and rearranging of information within a COMPUTER, and the subsequent transformation of that information by the computer's systems.

DEBENTURE

A type of BOND, issued by a corporation, whose documentation is held by trustees on behalf of the purchasers. Debentures usually have a charge on some specific ASSETS of the COMPANY. If the debenture holders are not repaid, they can lay claim to those assets instead.

DEBTOR

A COMPANY or individual who owes money to a CREDITOR.

DEBUG

To remove the "bugs"—problems—from COMPUTERS. Perhaps because computers are seen as dehumanizing, the language of computers has become nonhuman. Fructiferous brand names (like Apple) abound, and there is an important piece of HARDWARE called a "mouse."

The idea that faults inside computer SOFTWARE are caused by little bugs is in the same vein. It is also apposite. The damage caused by a software fault can be on the same scale as that caused by ants eating through a giant sequoia tree.

DECENTRALIZATION

The process of distributing power away from the center of very large organizations and out to semiautonomous divisions. The idea was popularized by the two Alfreds.

- Alfred Chandler, the business historian, whose book *Strategy and Structure* looked at decentralization as a corporate STRUCTURE particularly suited to the geographically and commercially diversified CONGLOMERATES that grew up after World War II.

- Alfred Sloan, the chairman for many years of General Motors, whose book *My Years with General Motors* described putting into effect what he called "federal decentralization" at the then fast-growing car company in the 1920s.

Chandler's book came out in 1962, Sloan's in 1963. For the rest of that decade companies busily considered how best to decentralize. For the most part, however, they took decentralization only so far. Operational responsibilities were devolved to divisional managers in the field, but strategic management was maintained firmly at the center: a combination of centralization and decentralization within the same organization.

DECISION TREE

A graphic representation of the various options flowing from an initial decision. A decision tree might, for example, be drawn up by a MERCHANT BANKER reviewing the possible courses of action following a takeover bid; a number of branches will spread out from each "decision point," creating the effect of a tree.

DEFAULT

The failure to repay a debt on time. Once a DEBTOR is in default, a lender has the right to follow legal processes to recover its loan.

DEFERRED TAX

The financial statements that a COMPANY prepares for its shareholders are not the same as those that it prepares for the tax inspector and on which its tax bill is assessed. There are certain things that accountants may net out of their calculation of PROFIT—such as transfers to reserves for future rainy days—which the tax inspector will want to add back for the calculation of taxable profit.

On the other hand, there are some things in the accountants' profit on which the tax inspector may postpone payment of tax. In such instances the company may set aside profits in its accounts to pay "deferred tax" at the later date on which it becomes due.

DEMAND

Together with SUPPLY and price, the raw materials of the science of economics: the willingness of individuals to pay a price for something. How agreeable they are can be demonstrated by drawing a graph of quantity against price.

In the 1980s economic theory was dominated by the so-called supply-siders whose political incarnations were Ronald Reagan and Margaret Thatcher. They were reacting to the demand-side theories of JOHN MAYNARD KEYNES, who maintained that fiddling with tax rates and the level of public spending to adjust demand in an economy was all a government needed to do to fine-tune employment and production.

DEMOGRAPHICS

The distribution of human populations according to age, sex, race, and so on. An important part of MARKETING any product or service is a knowledge of the demographics of the MARKET in which it is to be sold. It is no good trying to sell yogurt to people who cannot digest milk products. Clever marketing often depends on spotting demographic changes at an early stage. Two recent demographic changes have provided some exciting marketing opportunities.

- A sharp fall in the birth rate in many developed countries. This has led some northern European nations to experience a decline in their total population. In other words, there are fewer births than deaths, a situation unknown in Europe since World War II. Combined with an increase in longevity, this has turned marketers' attention away from the cult of youth to the cult of age. Growth industries have been in leisure and in health care.

- A shrinking in the average size of the family unit. This has come about because of the high divorce rate, later marriage, and the greater mobility of individuals. It has provided **MARKETING** opportunities in the food industry for things like ready meals for singles.

Depreciation

Also known as amortization, an amount that is charged against the **PROFITS** of a **COMPANY** to take account of the fact that some of its fixed **ASSETS** are wearing out and will have to be replaced. It allows accountants to spread the **COST** of things like plant and equipment over a number of years, instead of charging them all against the profit of the year in which they are bought.

Depreciation is probably the most inconsistently applied accounting standard in the world.

Center for International Financial Analysis and Research

Deregulation

Literally the removal of regulations. In the 1980s deregulation became a sort of faith that cemented the supply-side economists of the Reagan and Thatcher years. Among the first industries to

be deregulated under their influence was that of the U.S. airlines. Rules governing the routes that airlines could fly and the
prices that they could charge were lifted. For a while there was
a flurry of activity. Ten years later, however, the industry re-
sembled nothing so much as its pre-deregulation self.

A not dissimilar analysis can be applied to other industries
that have been enthusiastically deregulated, such as banking. In
telecommunications, on the other hand, there has not yet been
enough deregulation of state monopolies.

DESIGN

A vital ingredient in the industrial process: the arranging of
the appearance of a product. Design is more important to some
industries than others. Obviously in fashion and jewelry it is
the difference between success and failure. It is also crucial to
the car, hotel, and publishing industries. With perfumes, the
design of the bottle and of the packaging invariably costs several
times as much as the perfume itself.

DESKTOP PUBLISHING

A specialized development of COMPUTER technology (closely associated with Apple) that has turned almost every COMPANY
into a publisher. With a personal computer and a small number
of SOFTWARE programs almost anybody can prepare a publication to the stage where it is ready to be printed.

The power of desktop publishing has resulted in a welter of
in-house company publications and the simultaneous destruction of any residual belief that the computer would create a
"paperless society." The need now is for companies to concen-
trate on the purpose of their publications and to stop wallowing
in their ability to produce them.

DEVALUATION

A word that used to be on every businessman's lips in the days
of fixed EXCHANGE RATES: a sudden downward adjustment in

the VALUE of a country's currency against another currency. Devaluations usually occurred at weekends amid much drama.

Under the Bretton Woods Agreement of 1944 exchange rates between currencies were fixed and could only be changed by mutual agreement. But as countries' trade got out of balance (that is, they imported more than they exported), they forgot about mutual agreement and devalued to increase the local price of their imports. Once one country did this, other countries' trade then went out of balance. So they also devalued, and this cascade of "competitive devaluation" soon made the original one useless.

The Bretton Woods Agreement was abandoned in the early 1970s and exchange rates floated more freely. The European Monetary System, however, re-established a less rigid, semi-fixed exchange rate regime among the members of the EUROPEAN COMMUNITY.

DEVELOPMENT

See RESEARCH AND DEVELOPMENT

DIFFERENTIATION

The process of making a product or service seem superior to or different from its competitors' so that CONSUMERS ask specifically for it (by its brand name) rather than for just anything that serves the same purpose. Thus when shoppers ask for a jar of Maxwell House rather than for a jar of instant coffee, Maxwell House has successfully differentiated its product.

Differentiation can be established through any of the four Ps.

The product itself

The price

The promotion. The way it is sold. A product introduced as "low-fat" may, for example, be no different from (and no less fattening than) a rival launched at a time when consumers

were less weight conscious. Nevertheless, its proclaimed
slimming qualities will differentiate it in consumers' eyes.

The place. Where it is sold. A cheese sold only in delicatessens,
for example, can be priced higher than an identical cheese
sold only at supermarkets. The cheese in the supermarket
will, of course, be hoping to gain from a higher volume of
sales.

DIGITAL

The representation of data by a series of digits. Thus a digital
clock gives the time in the form of four digits (for example,
15:32), not as a pair of hands pointing at numbers on a face.

In a digital COMPUTER, information is transmitted as a series
of digits. In an analog computer, some variable physical quality
(such as electric voltage) represents the data. This allows analog
computers to function much quicker than digital ones.

DIMINISHING MARGINAL UTILITY

A long-winded phrase for one of those "laws" that dresses up
simple observations in convoluted language. The law of diminishing marginal utility says that the more you consume, the
less you want to consume. Every unit consumed gives less satisfaction than the one before.

Such a law might raise the eyebrows of ordinary mortals.
They know that a swig of whisky can increase the desire for
another swig, and they know that the last chocolate is not always the least pleasing.

DIMINISHING RETURNS

The economic principle that as more resources are put into a
project, the less are the resulting increases in output. When
workers start a job they are reasonably productive; as they
"warm up" they reach their peak productivity; then, as they get
tired, the law of diminishing returns sets in. For every hour's

work they do thereafter they produce less. Diminishing returns are almost the opposite of ECONOMIES OF SCALE and, indeed, are sometimes known as diseconomies of scale.

DIRECT COST

A COST that is directly attributable to the production of a product—the cost of steel for a car manufacturer, for instance. The direct cost varies in direct proportion to the number of units produced and is to be contrasted with OVERHEADS.

DIRECTIVE

A key document in the process of EUROPEAN COMMUNITY law making. Directives are issued by the European Commission to governments of member states, "directing" them to introduce into their national legislation laws that the EC has passed.

These laws are passed after the Commission has produced several "draft directives," which are circulated for comment to the likes of industry associations and CONSUMER-protection groups. The Commission is obliged also to consider the opinion of the European Parliament on draft directives. Directives lose their draft status when the Council of Ministers has agreed to pass them into law.

DIRECT MAIL

A method of selling goods and SERVICES by sending catalogues, leaflets, and order literature through the mail. Sometimes known as "junk mail," there is a (false) belief that nobody reads direct mail on its way from the mailman's bag to the trash. If it were so ineffective, would firms like *Readers's Digest* continue to use it so extensively?

DIRECTOR

A person appointed by shareholders to look after their interests in the MANAGEMENT of their COMPANY. The directors as a body constitute the BOARD of a company.

Company directors are restricted in what they can do. In general, they cannot make CONTRACTS with the company, and they cannot take loans from the company (unless it is in the business of making loans, like a bank). Somebody who is declared bankrupt can only continue to be a director with the special permission of the court. If a company is deemed to have been trading when it was technically insolvent, directors can become personally liable for its debts. One of the few benefits for directors is that they are free effectively to determine their own remuneration.

The term director is also used loosely, particularly in the United States, in the titles of senior management posts, for example, MARKETING director, personnel director. Such "directors" may well not have a seat on the board.

I emphasize the importance of details. You must perfect every fundamental of your business if you expect it to perform well.

Ray Kroc, founder of McDonald's

DISCOUNT

A reduction in the stated price of something. A discount can be offered for many reasons.

- A financial instrument may be sold at a discount to its face VALUE because the fixed rate of interest it pays is below the MARKET rate. When market interest rates are 10%, a $1,000 government BOND with a 5% coupon (the rate of interest attached to it) will sell for $500—that is, at a 50% discount.
- Vendors may give a discount for prompt payments in cash (a "cash discount"). Credit card companies fought hard for years to prevent RETAILERS that accepted their cards from giving cash discounts.

- Vendors often give a quantity discount that varies with the quantity of goods purchased. They can also give what is known as a "trade discount" to retailers or wholesalers in the same trade: garment manufacturers to dress shops, for example.

DISCOUNTED CASH FLOW

A method of calculating the present VALUE of a future stream of income and CAPITAL (the "cash flow"). Discounted cash flow (DCF) is used to compare different expected RATES OF RETURN on different projects.

It is based on discounting back future flows of cash in order to find their NET PRESENT VALUE. Suppose an investment of $100 in project A is expected to bring in $10 at the end of one year and $110 at the end of two years. On the other hand, investing $100 in project B is expected to bring in nothing at the end of year one, but $125 at the end of year two. Which project gives the better rate of return?

DISCRIMINATION

The practice of treating one set of things differently from another. Although economists talk of price discrimination (charging a different price for the same product in different markets), most talk of discrimination is of the sexual and racial kind. In developed countries it is illegal for a COMPANY to discriminate in any way on the grounds of a person's race or sex.

In the United States a number of companies have a policy of "positive discrimination." This entails employing more women and black people than is justified by their proportions in the general population in order to rectify past discrimination.

DISINTERMEDIATION

The process whereby financial intermediaries (like banks) get chopped out of the chain that passes money from an original lender to an ultimate borrower. Disintermediation is encouraged by the large margins that banks maintain on their lending. It has accelerated recently for the following reasons:

- The creation and growth of new financial instruments like commercial paper has encouraged companies to invest their short-term cash in tradable instruments rather than in bank deposits.

- Companies have begun to lend directly among themselves: from COMPANY B, which has surplus cash, to company A, which does not.

DISK DRIVE

That part of a COMPUTER that drives the machinery for recording and reading information stored on disks. (Floppy disks are the magnetic flat plates inserted into slits in the front or side of computers; hard disks refer to memory devices *inside* the computer.)

DISTRIBUTION CHANNELS

The routes, both physical and managerial, by which a product travels from manufacturer to CONSUMER. So integrated is the world's economy nowadays that any product can be distributed anywhere at almost any time. Fresh flowers in Paris on a winter's day were growing in Madagascar at the beginning of the week; apples in New York in December were on a branch in Chile in November.

Gasp inducing as these facts (and the managerial and technical skills required to bring them about) are, there must be physical limits to the distribution of products around the world. Some of these can already be seen on major roads in Europe, for example. A full COST-BENEFIT ANALYSIS of the Italian strawberry on the Berlin housewife's springtime breakfast table has not yet been carried out.

DIVERSIFICATION

A currently unpopular corporate STRATEGY that ensures a COMPANY does not have all its eggs in one basket. Diversification starts with the production of a product that has little to do with a company's existing product range. Bic, for example, the inventor of the ball-point pen, diversified into the disposable razor business.

Many companies have come to grief by diversification. In *In Search of Excellence,* published in 1982, Tom Peters and Robert Waterman emphasized "the almost total absence of any rigorous support for very diversified business combinations." Yet at the time, few paid attention.

Nowadays the popular strategy is to "stick to your knitting"; in other words, do more of what you are good at. Those companies that have diversified successfully have usually done so in some way that was related to their existing MARKETS. They have used the same distribution channels (for example, a company manufacturing handbags has diversified into making belts), or they have sold the same products into new markets (for example, a restaurant has diversified into providing a take-out service).

DIVESTMENT

The opposite of DIVERSIFICATION. Companies eliminate certain businesses or operations that do not fit with their mainstream strategy.

DIVIDEND

The amount of a COMPANY'S annual PROFIT that is set aside for the company's shareholders. A company may decide to pay an "interim dividend" in the middle of the fiscal year as a sort of advance on the full-year payment.

When a company has had a good year, the dividend payment should be high, and vice versa, but too often things do not work out like that. Shareholders expect dividends to increase every year without fail, rather like an indexed interest payment. Companies dare not frustrate the expectations of these shareholders turned bondholders for fear of the effect they might have on their SHARE price.

Shares are sometimes sold on the STOCK MARKET "cum dividend," meaning that the price for the share includes the company's next dividend payment (which has probably been announced but not yet paid). (See also INTEREST COVER)

DOCUMENTARY CREDIT

A method of financing trade in which importers of goods get credit from a bank on the basis of documents that prove that the goods are rightly theirs. This enables them to pay the vendors for the goods before they sell them themselves. Documentary credits have been assisted by the growth of FAX machines and international courier services, both of which enable documents to travel much faster than goods.

DOGS

One of the squares in the famous BOSTON MATRIX, dogs are companies with a low MARKET SHARE in a low-growth sector. The first reaction they invoke is that they should quickly be disposed of; the least they demand is some attention and strategic change.

DOUBLE ENTRY

The fundamental principle of BOOKKEEPING, and therefore of accounting, that every entry in a COMPANY'S books has an equal and opposite counterpart. Every transaction that a company effects creates an asset on one side of the ledger and an equal and opposite liability on the other side.

This duality of business transactions means that a company's books must always balance; that is, the monetary VALUE of each side of the ledger must be equal. This is the origin of the expression "**BALANCE SHEET.**" Double-entry bookkeeping has been around for centuries; its early development is usually attributed to fourteenth-century Italians.

DOUBLE-LOOP LEARNING

A concept closely associated with the writing of Chris Argyris on **ORGANIZATIONAL BEHAVIOR.** Single-loop learning is what happens when employees correct errors without changing the corporate norms that caused the error in the first place. Double-loop learning occurs when errors are corrected by examining and altering the norms first, and then fixing the erroneous action. Only that way does the **COMPANY** continue to benefit from the lesson that the employee who handled the problem learned even after the employee is gone.

DOUBLE-TAXATION AGREEMENT

When companies start to trade in a number of countries, they can find themselves liable to tax in more than one jurisdiction. A **COMPANY** will normally be liable for domestic tax on all its worldwide **PROFIT**, no matter where it arises. It may also owe tax on that same profit in the country in which it is incurred.

To help companies avoid being taxed twice on the same profit in two different places, many pairs of countries have so-called double-taxation agreements between themselves. These are often very complicated and deal with much more than company profits. They may include, for example, provisions to avoid the double taxation of income, **DIVIDENDS** or interest payments. The agreements normally allow companies that have been taxed on profits in the country where they arose to deduct those taxes from their tax bill in their country of residence. Moreover, when there is no double-taxation agreement, companies can often treat the tax paid abroad as a deductible expense when calculating their domestic taxable profit.

DOUBTFUL DEBT

A COMPANY'S debts are either good, bad, or doubtful. They are good if they still fall within the agreed repayment period, or within the period (30, 60, or 90 days) that is standard for the industry. If they are still unpaid beyond that period, they become doubtful. Companies then put aside an amount of their PROFIT against the possibility that the debt (which is in their books as an ASSET) will not be repaid.

Some companies go through each individual doubtful debt and assess the likelihood of its being repaid. Others simply set aside a percentage (based on industry experience) of all their doubtful debts.

A debt becomes bad when the person or company who owes it goes BANKRUPT, or has no possibility of repaying. The company then has to "write off" the debt and deduct the entire amount from its profits.

DOWNMARKET

A MARKETING term that assumes that MARKETS have a top and a bottom, and that products continually move "UPMARKET" toward the top, or "downmarket" toward the bottom. It is not always clear what scale this top and bottom are on: Is it the price of the product, the social class of the buyer, or the exclusivity of the product? Is a basic Rolls-Royce car a downmarket product? Is every shop in Gstaad or Vail upmarket?

DOWNSIDE RISK

The worst possible outcome of a MANAGEMENT decision. If a COMPANY invests $100 million in a new business, the downside risk may be much higher. The business may close, incurring layoff COSTS; there may be decommissioning costs if plants must be closed down; and there might even be intangible losses from being seen by the COMPETITION to have failed.

DOWNTIME

Originally the amount of paid time that employees spent not working because they lacked the necessary materials or because their machinery was being serviced. In established European and U.S. plants this could be as much as 20% of the working week.

Japanese methods of production have reduced the amounts of downtime to an absolute minimum, and the word has taken on a new meaning in the world of COMPUTERS. There it refers to the amount of time lost because a computer is not working, expressed as a percentage of the total amount of time it was planned that it should work.

DUTCH AUCTION

An auction in which the auctioneer starts by asking a high price that is gradually lowered until a buyer is found. The wonderful Dutch flower auctions are organized in this way. It is the opposite of most auctions held more than 50 miles from Amsterdam. In a non-Dutch auction, it is the last bidder who gets the lot on sale; in a Dutch auction the first bidder gets it.

DUTIES

Taxes on particular goods or SERVICES. Duties are roughly divided into the following two types:

Excise duties. Imposed on goods or services produced within the country that is levying the tax. Excise duties are popularly imposed on alcohol, tobacco, and gasoline. There are also things called stamp duties, which are paid when SHARES or property are sold, and death duties, which are imposed on the property of the recently deceased.

Import duties. Imposed on goods brought into a country (often called TARIFFS). The so-called duty-free shops found at airports and border posts are a misnomer. The prices of goods (alcohol, tobacco, watches, perfume, and so on) sold there are far higher than they would be if there were no duty on them whatsoever.

EARNOUT

A compromise between what vendors believe their companies' future profit will be and what purchasers expect them to be. An earnout is a way of paying for a COMPANY based on its future performance. The purchase price is a combination of an immediate up-front payment plus a number of future payments related to future performance.

EC

See EUROPEAN COMMUNITY

ECONOMETRICS

The application of mathematics to economics. Econometricians (and the COMPUTERS that they rely on) develop complicated equations that attempt to define the relationships between different variables in an economy such as savings, growth, INFLATION, and so on.

Most econometrics today is concerned with what is called "macroeconomics" (the study of whole economies) and not "microeconomics" (the study of parts of economies, like businesses). So economists' and econometricians' main contribution to managers is to describe and forecast the background economic climate in which they must operate.

In all recorded history there has not been one economist who has had to worry about where the next meal is coming from.

Peter Drucker

ECONOMIC AND MONETARY UNION

The process of integrating the currencies and monetary policies of the 12 member states of the EUROPEAN COMMUNITY. Economic and monetary union (EMU) began in the early 1970s with something called "the snake," a managed EXCHANGE-RATE system that aimed to limit fluctuations between EC currencies.

The snake effectively died in 1976, but three years later a new European Monetary System (EMS) was born. It was based on something called the EUROPEAN CURRENCY UNIT (ecu).

In the Exchange-Rate Mechanism (ERM) of the EMS, European currencies can fluctuate within a given percentage of their rate against the ecu. Should they threaten to break outside the percentage band (and there are two bands, a wide one for weaker currencies and a narrow one for stronger ones), then central banks agree to intervene, buying or selling currencies to adjust the rates. Should that not be enough, then governments have to adjust interest rates or other internal economic variables.

By the late 1980s continental Europe was keen to take the process of monetary union further. At a meeting in Maastricht at the end of 1991 the Community provisionally agreed to take a number of steps.

1991–1994. Completion of the first stage of EMU, with greater integration of EC monetary and economic policies. All member states will come within the narrow band of the EMS' EXCHANGE-RATE mechanism.

January 1, 1994. The second stage of EMU begins. The composition of the basket of currencies in the ecu is frozen, and a European Monetary Institute (EMI) is set up to coordinate the member states' monetary policy.

End–1996. A report on progress will show how far the member states' economies have converged in terms of INFLATION, interest rates, and budget deficits. On the basis of this report it will be decided when and how to move to the third stage of

EMU, in which member states will share a single currency and a single European central bank.

ECONOMIES OF SCALE

The average COST of a manufactured unit decreases when more units are manufactured. For example, if it costs $X to make 10 cars, it costs much less than $2X to make 20 cars because much of the expense involved in making the first 10 does not have to be repeated to make another 10. Such "economies of scale" lie behind all MASS PRODUCTION and help to make highly sophisticated products available to many.

There are limits to economies of scale. The bigger a plant becomes, the more unmanageable it is. The cost of this unmanageability eventually outweighs the benefits from economies of scale. The president of Motorola, the American electronics firm, once said, "When a plant starts to edge toward 1,500 people, somehow, like magic, things start to go wrong."

ECONOMIES OF SCOPE

This is a variation on the thinking behind ECONOMIES OF SCALE. Economies of scope are savings gained from producing a wider range of products to funnel through an existing DISTRIBUTION CHANNEL.

ECU

See EUROPEAN CURRENCY UNIT

EEA

See EUROPEAN ECONOMIC AREA

EFTA

See EUROPEAN FREE TRADE ASSOCIATION

EIB

See EUROPEAN INVESTMENT BANK

ELASTICITY

An economic concept of considerable significance, elasticity is a measure of the relationship between two variables: how much one changes depending on changes in the other. For example, take the price elasticity of demand. If a 1% change in the price of an item results in more than a 1% change in demand, then the relationship is elastic. If the price change were less than 1%, the relationship would be said to be inelastic.

ELECTRONIC MAIL

The transmission of electronic "letters" from one COMPUTER to another. The computers have to be linked to telecommunications systems by means of a MODEM, which translates computer signals into telecom signals. On arrival at their destination, the signals are translated back into computerese by another modem.

The growth in electronic mail has been less than its potential once suggested it might be. It has certainly not put paper mills out of business. People like to see a "hard copy" of the information they receive. The great majority of electronic messages are put into print upon receipt.

EMBARGO

A ban on something, for example, a government-imposed ban on trading with a particular country (e.g., with Iraq after it invaded Kuwait).

EMPLOYMENT AGENCIES

PUBLIC-SECTOR and PRIVATE-SECTOR bodies that attempt to match the supply of LABOR with demand. Some agencies specialize in supplying particular industries or skills; others in supplying temporary replacements ("temps") for jobs that are only va-

cant for a short time. Employment agents for top managers are
called "headhunters."

EMPLOYMENT CONTRACT

The formal agreement between an employer and an employee
laying down the terms and conditions of employment in the
COMPANY. In most developed countries it is now illegal to discriminate between employees; they must have the same CON-
TRACT for the same work.

EMPOWERMENT

An idea associated largely with the work of Rosabeth Moss
Kanter, a sociologist/MANAGEMENT teacher who argues that
only those companies that can "empower" all individuals (give
them the power to act on their own initiative) in the workplace
stand a chance of winning in the "corporate Olympics" of the
1990s. Too many employees still need the "crutch" of HIERAR-
CHY to empower them.

---

*The powerless live in a different world . . . they
may turn to the ultimate weapon of those who
lack productive power: oppressive power.*

Rosabeth Moss Kanter

EMU

See ECONOMIC AND MONETARY UNION

ENTERPRISE

Either a business organization (as in "state enterprise") or an
economic system in which people are free to do business more
or less as they wish (as in "free enterprise"). Or the quality

exemplified by the risk-taking businessman (as in "Sam Walton showed great enterprise in setting up Wal-Mart stores"). Whichever it is, successful economies cannot do without it.

> *I reckon one entrepreneur can recognize another at 300 yards on a misty day.*
> Sir Peter Parker, a former chairman of British Rail

ENTREPRENEUR

A term that started off with a specific economic meaning: the person who organizes the factors of production (land, LABOR, and CAPITAL), the RISK taker in business. Some economists consider the entrepreneur to be a fourth factor of production, without which the other three cannot produce anything. These economists, however, cannot have seen Europe's nationalized industries, many of which carry on producing without an entrepreneur in sight.

The term has come to have a wider meaning, referring to anybody with the qualities of leadership and adaptability that are considered necessary to create wealth. Much effort has gone into trying to identify these people, to nurture and encourage them with tax breaks, and to support them within large organizations (leading to a new expression, INTRAPRENEURSHIP).

> *I think if we want to understand the entrepreneur, we should look at the juvenile delinquent.*
> Abraham Zaleznik, Harvard Business School

ENVIRONMENT

There are two meanings.

1. The commercial conditions in which a business operates. The number and nature of its competitors, the nature of its MARKET (growing or declining, large volume or niche), its workforce, and its plant. This environment shapes a COMPANY'S STRATEGY, and is also shaped by it. The Boston Consulting Group invented something called an Environments Matrix (see BOSTON MATRIX), which presents a framework for deciding which environments it is strategically sensible for a business to enter.

2. The environment in which the human race lives. This is increasingly being endangered by the side effects of industrialization. The way in which industry learns to live at peace with this environment is sure to be a key issue for the 1990s.

One of the best-kept secrets in America is that people are aching to make a commitment, if only they had the freedom and environment in which to do so.

John Naisbitt

ENVIRONMENTAL AUDIT

An attempt to use the checks and balances of auditing to assess the CONTROL that a COMPANY has over its impact on the ENVIRONMENT. The International Chamber of Commerce (ICC) defines an environmental AUDIT as "a MANAGEMENT tool comprising a systematic, documented, periodic, and objective evaluation of how well environmental organization, management, and equipment are performing."

The idea is a fairly new one, born out of "green consciousness," though some companies (like Shell Oil) have been carrying out environmental audits for more than a decade. Shell says that a successful environmental audit requires the following:

- Full management commitment
- Careful selection of the audit team to ensure objectivity
- Well-defined systematic procedures
- The preparation of written reports
- Quality assurance
- Follow-up

EQUAL OPPORTUNITIES

The idea that all men and women should have the same chance to climb the corporate ladder. Although many countries have legislation to enforce equal opportunities, there are still inequalities between men and women in the workforce.

On the shopfloor women have used equal opportunities legislation to get the same rate of pay for the same job as men and for the right to work the same (more highly paid) overtime as men. (In some countries, for instance, it has long been illegal for women to work at night.)

At more senior management levels women have been held back by the so-called glass ceiling. Nobody can yet say that women and men have an equal opportunity to be chief executive of General Motors.

EQUITY

The financial interest of shareholders in their COMPANY. In accounting terms that means the VALUE of the company's ASSETS minus its LIABILITIES. On a BALANCE SHEET this is referred to as "shareholders' funds." This equity is divided "equitably" among shareholders according to the number of SHARES they hold.

ERGONOMICS

The study of the way people work and how they can be improved to make a workforce more productive. Although the actual word "ergonomics" was not coined until 1950, the field of study it described was initially an outcrop of scientific MANAGEMENT, the early theories of management propounded by FREDERICK TAYLOR in which LABOR was seen as little more than a sophisticated machine.

Ergonomics looked specifically at the relationship between the human machine and its ENVIRONMENT. It concentrated on designing equipment to suit common physical characteristics and ways of relieving, for example, the pain and tedium of sitting for long periods in fixed positions. The subject then developed beyond these purely physical concerns to include psychological factors that affect people at work.

ETHICAL INVESTMENT

An increasingly powerful movement that maintains that investors have a moral duty (to invest in ethical companies) as well as a financial duty (to invest in companies that will give them the best rate of return).

The idea of ethical investment was boosted by two events in particular.

- The horror of Americans in general (and of black Americans in particular) at apartheid in South Africa. This led to pressure on investors to avoid companies that had businesses in South Africa.
- The green movement, which made investors more conscious of the environmental damage caused by their industries.

EUROMARKET

Financial MARKETS in currencies held outside the country that issued them, usually dollars held outside the United States or deutschemarks held outside Germany, called Eurodollars and Eurodeutschemarks, respectively.

These currencies are held with banks in financial centers like London, Luxembourg, Hong Kong, and the Cayman Islands, where there are fewer regulations than in the United States or Germany. (So banks there can pay better rates for deposits since regulation always has a COST.)

Another advantage to these markets is that there is less chance of the deposits being frozen for political reasons, as has occurred on occasion with foreign deposits in the United States.

EUROPEAN COMMUNITY

The European Community (EC) is the combination of three international communities created by Western Europe in the aftermath of World War II. The communities, largely forged by political idealists like Jean Monnet, were an attempt to bind Europe together in such a way that it could never again go to war within itself. The three communities were the EEC, the European Economic Community; Euratom, a community for nuclear research; and the ECSC, the European Coal and Steel Community.

The original six members of the EC (Belgium, France, Italy, Luxembourg, the Netherlands, and West Germany) have, since they signed the binding Treaty of Rome in 1957, been joined by six others: Denmark, Greece, Ireland, Portugal, Spain, and the United Kingdom.

So far the focus of the Community has been largely on economic union, aiming to create a "common market" and then a "single market." In late 1991 the Community provisionally committed itself to monetary union by the end of the century and to various other measures that would imply closer political union.

Most of the EC's infrastructure is based in Brussels.

• The European Commission, based in the distinctive Berlaymont building (which may soon be knocked down), is the executive organ of the Community.

• The European Parliament, which spreads itself between Brussels, Strasbourg, and Luxembourg, is an assembly of elected politicians from around the Community. It has a largely consultative role in the EC law-making process.

• The Council of Ministers is the body that decides whether to proceed with legislation proposed by the Commission. It is made up of national ministers from each member state who meet according to the issues involved. For example, the common agricultural policy (CAP), one of the EC's biggest early policy initiatives, is determined by a council of all 12 national ministers of agriculture.

EUROPEAN CURRENCY UNIT

The denomination that dedicated Europeans hope will become a single European currency, accepted in shops from Aberdeen to Lisbon.

The European currency unit (ecu) was originally a technical creation that existed only on paper. It was a theoretical basket of European currencies—a few pence added to a few francs plus a bit of a deutschemark, and so on—the amount of each currency in the basket determined by the size of the economy that issued it. Countries that participated in the European Monetary System then set their EXCHANGE RATE in terms of this ecu.

Gradually the ecu began to be used in commercial transactions. The European Commission denominates its invoices in ecus; some banks offer ecu deposits and ecu loans; and, for a short while, shops in part of Luxembourg quoted all their prices in ecus.

EUROPEAN ECONOMIC AREA

European Economic Area (EEA) is a term used to describe the 19 countries of the EUROPEAN COMMUNITY and the 7 that belong to the EUROPEAN FREE TRADE ASSOCIATION. In October 1991 these two blocs agreed to set up a common MARKET embracing all their members. Its main features are as follows:

- Free movement of goods within the area from 1993
- Special arrangements covering food, fish, energy, coal, and steel
- EFTA to adopt EC rules on COMPANY law, consumer protection, education, the ENVIRONMENT, R&D, and social policy
- EFTA to adopt EC rules on competition, abuse of a dominant position, public procurement, mergers, and state aid
- An independent court to handle EFA disputes on competition policy
- Mutual recognition of qualifications throughout the EEA from 1993, and freedom to live and work anywhere in the area
- Switzerland to have an extra five years to remove its tight laws on immigration
- The freeing of capital movements, although CONTROLS will remain on some direct investment in EFTA and on some foreign purchases of EFTA real estate
- EFTA countries to be free to stay outside the EC's common agricultural policy

EUROPEAN FREE TRADE ASSOCIATION

A European trading bloc consisting of Austria, Finland, Iceland, Liechtenstein, Norway, Sweden, and Switzerland. The headquarters of the European Free Trade Association (EFTA) are in Geneva. Denmark, Portugal, and the United Kingdom were all members of EFTA until they were given a chance to join the EC.

EFTA is less ambitious than the EC. It has removed TARIFFS and quotas on goods moving from one member state to another, but each member retains its own tariffs against any third country's imports. The EC, on the other hand, has harmonized its tariffs against non-EC countries.

Much of the external trade of the two European communities (EFTA and the EC) is with each other, and there have been a number of treaties reducing TRADE BARRIERS between them. Several EFTA members have indicated that they would like to join the EC, and as time goes by the two blocs will in any case become closer, melding into a 19-nation unit that has already been christened the EUROPEAN ECONOMIC AREA.

EUROPEAN INVESTMENT BANK

The European Investment Bank (EIB) was created by the Treaty of Rome, the treaty that also established the EUROPEAN COMMUNITY. The EIB is a development bank that uses its good reputation to borrow cheaply on various international financial markets and then lends to borrowers within the EC and its associate member states (countries like Cyprus and Malta that are halfway to full membership). EIB loans are long term and have maturities of 7 to 12 years.

The bank has certain priority areas in its lending.

- Depressed regions, like most of Portugal and large parts of Ireland
- The development of European technology
- Joint infrastructure projects (like the Channel Tunnel) involving more than one member state

EXCELLENCE

A school of MANAGEMENT thinking clustered around (and inspired by) *In Search of Excellence,* the best-selling book by Tom Peters and Robert Waterman, published in 1982. The book marked a shift from thinking about management as a largely quantitative exercise in planning and efficiency to considering it a qualitative process aimed first and foremost at satisfying customers. It changed management from an introverted subject to an extroverted one.

There are no excellent companies.

Tom Peters, *Thriving on Chaos*

*World-class excellence is continual improvement
in serving the customer's four basic wants:
ever-better quality, ever-lower costs,
ever-increasing flexibility, and
ever-quicker response.*

Richard Schonberger

EXCHANGE CONTROL

Government rules on the amount of its currency that can be
taken out of a country or, in some instances, that can be brought
in. The most familiar sort of exchange CONTROL is imposed on
travelers at their entry or exit from certain countries. The more
significant form of exchange control, however, is imposed on
companies, and it limits their ability to finance trade or investment abroad with their own currency. The aim of exchange
controls is to support the EXCHANGE RATE (that is, the price) of
a nation's currency by limiting the sale of it.

In recent years governments have used interest rates rather
than exchange controls as the main economic tool for adjusting
exchange rates. Exchange controls went out of fashion for several reasons.

- The EUROMARKET grew as a location in which to keep currencies OFFSHORE. These currencies never came home and could
be used abroad whenever their owners wanted, regardless of
exchange controls.

- The free-market economics espoused by Margaret Thatcher
and Ronald Reagan was philosophically opposed to exchange
controls. The United Kingdom abolished virtually all its

(once extensive) exchange controls in 1979, the year that Margaret Thatcher came into office.

- The development of the EUROPEAN COMMUNITY depended on the removal of barriers to the free flow of CAPITAL among EC member states. This implied the complete removal of exchange controls, although some member states (like France and Italy) have been slow to comply with EC directives on this.

EXCHANGE RATE

The price at which one currency can be exchanged for another. The basic price for most currencies is expressed in dollars.

Exchange rates come in various forms.

Fixed rate. Governments fix the rate against something else: the price of gold, the dollar, or the ecu, for example. When it has to change the rate, a government does so either by a devaluation (increasing the amount of currency per dollar, ounce of gold, or whatever) or by a revaluation (decreasing the amount of currency per unit).

Floating rate. Governments allow their currency to find its own level according to demand in the foreign-exchange markets.

Forward rate. The exchange rate today for delivery of a currency at some future date. It removes risk for companies to buy currencies in the "forward MARKET" when they know that they have to pay large foreign-currency bills in the future. Forward rates are usually expressed as a premium (or DISCOUNT) on the spot rate.

Spot rate. The exchange rate for immediate delivery of a currency: "on the spot," as opposed to "forward." Will a currency that is too forward find itself on the spot?

Two-tier rate. Some countries (like South Africa) have a fixed rate for certain types of transactions (like trade) and a different rate for all other transactions.

Unofficial rate. In countries with a fixed rate there is frequently an illegal black market where currency is bought and sold freely. The price in the black market is called the unofficial rate.

EXCHANGE RISK

The risk that a business takes when it buys or sells goods or SERVICES at prices denominated in a currency other than its own. For exporters this is normal practice, and there are ways for them to reduce the risk (to "hedge" it).

Exporters due to receive a payment in foreign currency at a future date can sell the currency forward at an agreed rate in exchange for their own currency. That reduces the intervening uncertainty. Many companies—from the very biggest to the very smallest—have come unstuck because they have preferred to take an exchange risk (in the hope of making a big gain from intervening shifts in exchange rates) rather than cover their foreign-exchange "exposure." If the EC adopts a common currency, the exchange risk of member countries' businesses will be reduced.

Executive: an ulcer with authority.

Fred Allen

EXPATRIATE

A favorite figure in literature (because so many writers are themselves expatriates?), the manager or skilled worker who is a foreigner in the country where he or she is working and living. Strictly speaking, an expatriate is sent abroad by her employer for a relatively short term, but that definition has been stretched to suit modern times. Expatriates nowadays may well be employed by the local SUBSIDIARY of a COMPANY that sent them abroad or, indeed, by a local company itself, for life.

Expatriates who are sent to live in unappealing places expect to get a number of generous perks (see FRINGE BENEFITS) to compensate—for example, regular free trips back home, school fees for their children, or various cost-of-living allowances. In general, the less pleasant the destination, the more perks the employee gets. One large firm of accountants estimates it costs three times as much to send a person to Moscow as it does to send them to Paris.

EXPERT SYSTEM

A highly sophisticated COMPUTER program that works on a detailed body of knowledge in a small specialist area and comes as close to reproducing human thought processes as is possible for a computer.

EXPORT CREDIT AGENCY

A government (or quasi-government) agency that does one or both of the following two things:

- Lends money to foreign buyers to buy goods from the country in which the agency is based. When the country is keen to boost exports, these loans are offered at SUBSIDIZED rates.

- Guarantees loans from banks to the domestic exporter. Such loans finance the transaction until the exporter is paid.

The United States's export credit agency is called Ex-Im Bank, France's is Coface, Germany's is Hermes, and the United Kingdom's is the Export Credits Guarantee Department (ECGD). To prevent these agencies from cut-throat COMPETITION, countries have agreed on what are called "consensus rates." These are interest rates that define the extent to which agencies can subsidize loans to purchase their own country's exports.

*If we take care of our imports, our exports will
take care of themselves.*

Anon

EXPORT CREDIT INSURANCE

A form of insurance taken out by exporters to cover their risk
between the time that they ship goods to a customer and the
time that they receive payment for the goods. Such insurance
can be obtained from either an EXPORT CREDIT AGENCY in the
form of a guarantee to a bank for loans given to the exporter, or
(to a more limited extent) private insurance companies that, for
a fee, will cover the risk of nonpayment.

EXPORT FINANCE

There are particular risks attached to financing exports that do
not arise with domestic trade. In developed economies special
state-backed insurers (like the Ex-Im Bank) provide cover
against these risks so that they do not discourage exporters from
trying to sell abroad.

The risks covered include the following:

- A unilateral breach of CONTRACT by a PUBLIC-SECTOR buyer,
  including nonpayment
- The frustration of a contract concluded with a private buyer
  for political or administrative reasons
- The inconvertibility or nontransfer of currency preventing
  the completion of an international trade deal
- The withdrawal or nonrenewal of a license preventing the
  performance of a trade deal
- The unfair calling of BONDS, performance bonds, or retention
  monies

- An ARBITRATION award refusal
- The EMBARGO, seizure, or confiscation of goods

EXPORT LICENSE

A document obtained from an official body allowing the export of goods that it is otherwise forbidden to take out of a country. Most countries require such licenses for the export of antiques, works of art, and military equipment, or for any goods that may be used for military purposes.

EXTRAORDINARY ITEM

This is exactly what it says: an item in a COMPANY'S financial statements that is out of the ordinary. What constitutes extraordinary, however, is not so simple. By and large, extraordinary items are revenues and expenses that do not come from the normal course of a company's operations and should therefore appear after the key figure of net PROFIT has been calculated. That creates a great temptation for companies to call all revenue items ordinary and all expenditure items extraordinary.

Factor cost

A pure, unsullied sort of cost that measures the price paid for the factors of production—land, LABOR, and CAPITAL—that is, rent for land, wages for labor, and interest or DIVIDENDS for capital. Added together, these prices give the total factor cost of an article. This differs from the MARKET price, for it excludes any subsidies received for production, and it ignores any taxes paid during production or imposed on consumption (like VAT).

Gross domestic product (GDP), the measure of a nation's output, is calculated either according to the market value of all the goods and SERVICES produced or (by adding back subsidies and subtracting taxes) according to the factor cost of all those goods and services.

Factoring

The practice of subcontracting to someone else (called the factor, and usually a financial COMPANY) the business of collecting money due on a company's invoices. There are two main reasons for factoring.

- The company is too small to efficiently run its own sales ledger (see BOOKKEEPING). In this case the factor will be paid a fee and will do everything from raising an invoice to chasing lax payers.

- The company is in need of cash and wants to accelerate payments due to it. In this case the factor "buys" the company's unpaid invoices at a DISCOUNT and then sets about collecting the money itself. This is a one-off operation, and the factor's fee is anything that it can collect above the discounted amount it paid for the invoices.

In this second type of factoring (sometimes known as invoice discounting) the company may not wish it to be known that it has sold its invoices (and is therefore in need of cash). In such cases the factor may continue to send out claims for payment in the company's name.

FACTORY

Originally a trading post in far-flung parts of the British Empire—like India and Canada—that was run by a "factor" (that is, an AGENT from Europe employed by the earliest large COMPANY, the East India Company, to run its trading posts). Factories, of course, are also places that use the economist's three "factors of production": LABOR, land, and CAPITAL.

The word factory came to conjure up images of chimney stacks, "satanic mills," and the exploitation of labor. This led to the various Factory Acts passed in the United Kingdom and the United States in the nineteenth century to protect the health and safety of factory workers.

FAMILY FIRM

The industrial wealth of all developed nations is built on the family business. Companies as big, as old, and as widely owned as Siemens, Barclays, and Fiat are still to a greater or lesser extent influenced by the offspring of the families that founded them. The heart of the vibrant small business sector is the family firm. The urge to "build up a business for the children" is no less strong now than it was 100 years ago.

STOCK MARKETS provide COMPANY founders with a pot of gold at the end of their toil, and the growth of stock markets has accelerated the evolution of companies from tightly held, family-run businesses into widely held and professionally managed corporations. The Martell family made its famous cognac continuously from 1715 until 1988. In that year the Canadian CONGLOMERATE, Seagram, offered the family FFr5.25 billion, which was 38 times Martell's previous year's earnings. It was an offer they could not refuse, and Martell is not a family firm anymore.

IMD, the business school in Lausanne, has gained a reputation for its teaching and research on the subject of family firms. It runs special courses looking at several aspects of the subject, including the following:

- The succession question
- Graceful exits
- Do nonfamily managers have to be owners as well?
- Extending the family to include daughters and sons-in-law (Raul Gardini was Ferruzzi's son-in-law; Henri Racamier was Vuitton's son-in-law; both transformed their family businesses into huge public companies.)
- Directors from outside the family
- Growth versus CAPITAL restraints

FAST TRACK

A special career path within an organization, designed for particularly able people who are not going to wait around until they have climbed all the steps of a normal career ladder to the top. The disadvantage of such a system is that it alienates those slower mortals who may, in the end, be the more able top managers.

FAX

The facsimile machine, perhaps the most commercially significant invention to come out of the last 40 years of the twentieth century. Known affectionately by its diminutive name, the facsimile machine scans a document of words or images and transmits them via telephone lines to another machine that converts the messages into a copy of the original document.

The fax has reinvented that great nineteenth-century service without which no Victorian novelist's plot would have gotten far: fast mail delivery. It is estimated that more than half the telephone calls between New York and Japan are now fax calls.

The machine has become so popular that it has bred "junk" fax: unsolicited messages transmitted much as junk mail is sent. If left on the specially sensitive fax paper, however, these messages can fade in as little as three months. Lawyers and all careful business people always take photocopies.

Japanese companies have obtained an extraordinarily high share of the world's MARKET for facsimile machines. That was in part due to a strategy of remorseless price cutting that created greater demand. That in turn enabled the manufacturers to make ECONOMIES OF SCALE and to cut prices further.

To me success can only be achieved through repeated failure and introspection. In fact, success represents the 1% of your work which results from the 99% that is called failure.

Soichiro Honda, founder of Honda

HENRI FAYOL

A Frenchman whose nineteenth-century ideas on MANAGEMENT were highly influential in the early decades of this century, although they seem to have little relevance to today's bigger and more complex industrial world. Born in 1841, Fayol spent virtually all his working life with a French coal-mining COMPANY. He started as an engineer and ended up as managing director for 30 years, turning the company from near disaster into the very model of industrial success.

His thinking was based on what became known as functionalism, a theory of organization that had a number of elements to it that were revolutionary then. They included the preparation of long-term plans of action, the regular production of management accounts, regular meetings of departmental heads, and the drawing up of organization charts that obeyed the two "unities": unity of command (one boss for every employee) and unity of direction (one boss and one plan for each business activity).

Fayol has been criticized for oversimplification arising from the simple nature of his one-product, unsophisticated, near-MONOPOLY business. Yet Fayol himself recognized that managers need to be flexible. "Rarely do we apply the same principle twice in identical situations," he once said.

FIFO

See FIRST IN, FIRST OUT

FINANCIAL YEAR

The 12-month period for which a COMPANY draws up its annual financial statements. This is not necessarily the calendar year January 1–December 31. Many companies close their financial year at the end of March, which is just as well. If all companies used the calendar year, auditors would be frantic in January, February, and March, and idle for the rest of the year.

Some companies choose more peculiar financial years (to the end of September, for example) for sound commercial reasons. Agricultural businesses may want their financial years to end when a seasonal harvest has been gathered and sold. Other companies sometimes have financial years that last longer than 12 months. Accounts can be drawn up for a 15-month period if, for example, a company wants to change the end of its financial year from September 30 to December 31. The reasons for doing this may be no more substantial than a desire to confuse shareholders by obscuring comparisons between one period and the next.

FIRING

The following guidelines should be adopted:

• All dismissals must be in accordance with employment law.

- If a disciplinary procedure exists, ensure it is adhered to.
- Allow employees to state their case.
- Investigate thoroughly before making a decision.
- In cases of alleged gross misconduct, suspend on full pay during investigation.
- Do not lose your temper; hasty words can be construed as a dismissal when none was intended.
- Keep written records of all stages of the procedure.

He was fired with enthusiasm because he wasn't fired with enthusiasm.

Anon

First in, first out

Commonly known by its acronym FIFO; a method of valuing stock-in-trade for accounting purposes. A **COMPANY** has a sizable stock of identical inputs to be used in production. They have been purchased at different times and at different prices. Are the most recent purchases being used up first, or the oldest? Since they are identical, you cannot tell merely by looking at them.

FIFO assumes that the oldest (probably those bought at the lowest price) are used up first, and this is the opposite of **LIFO** (**LAST IN, FIRST OUT**). FILO (first in, last out) is not a method of valuing stock; it is a description of the daily arrival and departure of the good leader.

Fisher equation

The equation MV = PT, where M is the quantity of money in circulation in an economy; V is the velocity at which it circulates (that is, how frequently it changes hands); P is the general price level; and T is the total volume of goods and SERVICES in the economy.

The equation was first formulated by an American economist, Irving Fisher, whose writing at the beginning of the twentieth century was influential in the development of mathematical economics and ECONOMETRICS. The equation is a simple way of expressing the quantity theory of money: the foundation of monetarism and of the relationship between prices, INFLATION, and the amount of money in an economy.

FIXED ASSET

An asset that remains in the business over time and is not merely being processed on its way from a supplier to a CONSUMER. Fixed assets include things like office buildings, factories, and land, but they are not necessarily fixed to the ground. Portable COMPUTERS are fixed assets to anybody but a portable computer manufacturer. The SHARES that a COMPANY owns in subsidiaries or associated companies are also fixed assets.

FIXED COST

A COST that does not vary with the amount of goods or SERVICES produced (the opposite of variable cost). Fixed costs are items like rent and bank interest: items that have to be paid regardless of whether anything is produced or sold. Philosophically there are no costs that are fixed in the long term, because in the long term, to quote one author, "any productive process is optional."

FLEXIBLE MANUFACTURING

Flexible is now a buzzword in all sorts of areas of business and MANAGEMENT. Only the flexible COMPANY will survive the 1990s, we are told. Its employees will work FLEXTIME (see below). They will have flexible workstations in a flexible organization that has introduced COMPUTER-aided flexible manufacturing systems

(FMS). And all of it will be financed, it is hoped, by a highly flexible line of credit.

Flexibility is a freedom created by the application of the computer to the administrative and productive functions of a company. Like all freedoms it can be abused, and like all freedoms it can confuse.

FLEXTIME

A schedule of work that allows employees to choose their own working hours around a "core time" at the middle of the day. Under this system employees who work an eight-hour day, for example, must work between, say, 11:00 a.m. and 3:00 p.m. They can then choose whether to work 7:00 a.m. to 3:00 p.m. or 11:00 a.m. to 7:00 p.m., to make up the eight hours.

Flextime only works where employees are involved in individual tasks, like architecture or door-to-door selling. It cannot be applied to jobs where continuous teamwork is required, or where (like teaching) the customer is only present within certain hours.

FLOATING CHARGE

A CHARGE that can be applied across all a COMPANY'S ASSETS. An unpaid CREDITOR with a floating charge has a right to claim any of the company's assets. A creditor with a fixed charge, on the other hand, has a right only to those assets (such as a building) that are specifically mentioned in the charge.

FLOATING-RATE NOTE

A debt instrument popular in the EUROMARKETS on which the interest rate is adjusted periodically to take account of changing MARKET conditions. The interest rate of floating-rate notes (FRNs) is often expressed with reference to some variable base point, frequently LIBOR (the London interbank offered rate), a variable rate that banks in London offer to pay each other for foreign currency deposits.

FLOPPY DISK

The disk that is inserted into computers in order to give them greater storage capacity or the ability to perform new tricks. In fact, floppy disk is fast becoming a misnomer. Disks used to flop and were 5¼ inches in diameter, but the standard size for the industry is changing. More and more disks are 3½ inches across, and they are "hard," not floppy.

FLOW OF FUNDS

A synonym for CASH FLOW. In some countries companies are required to publish a third statement in their annual financial statements along with their income statement and their BAL-ANCE SHEET. This is to show the flow of funds in and out of the COMPANY during an accounting period. In the United States this third statement is known as the Funds Flow Statement. In the United Kingdom it is known as the Source and Use of Funds.

FOB

See FREE ON BOARD

MARY PARKER FOLLETT

The first woman (described by one fan as a "gaunt Bostonian lady") to exert great influence on the study of MANAGEMENT. Follett's first book (with the unlikely title of *The Speaker of the House of Representatives*) was published in 1898 and was firmly based on her origins as a political scientist. But it had clear relevance to management, being a study of how effective particular speakers had been as leaders of the house, and why.

Follett's subsequent writing can be seen as a reaction to the mechanistic ideas of FREDERICK TAYLOR and of scientific management. She saw workers as fallible human beings, not sophisticated machines. The skill of management was to bring these human beings together into groups and to understand what could make them operate successfully.

By and large Follett's ideas have been better received in Japan (where there is a Follett Society for the appreciation of her work) than in the West, where her male audiences did not always take to her "soft," feminine approach to the business of men.

Management, not bankers nor stockholders, is the fundamental element in industry. It is good management that draws credit, that draws workers, that draws customers . . . Management is the permanent function of business.

Mary Parker Follett

FORECASTING

No business can get very far without making some guesses about what will happen in the future. These may be predictions about the general economy, about a COMPANY'S specific MARKETS, or about the supply and price of RAW MATERIALS that the company uses.

Most forecasts are based partly on extrapolations from past experiences. Since the past is never repeated, the prediction will almost certainly be wrong. A forecast (of something like PROFIT) that is based on previous ones will therefore almost certainly be wrong. Yet investors continue to be surprised when companies' formal "profit forecasts" do not come true.

Gilbert Heebner, an American economist, has drawn up a useful list of seven laws to take into account when forecasting (or when considering other people's forecasts).

1. The future is not random; but history does not repeat itself exactly either.

2. From time to time major (and usually unpredictable) shocks throw an economy off-course.

3. The consensus of economists' forecasts is more often right than wrong.

4. Sticking for too long to one economic theory can be dangerous to your health as a forecaster.

5. Economic forces work relentlessly but on an uncertain timetable. So, many forecasts may be correct in all but their timing.

6. Abnormalities are always significant.

7. The road is more important than the inn: there is more to be learned from the way in which the forecast was arrived at than from the forecast itself.

FOREIGN DIRECT INVESTMENT

The investment by residents of one country in the industries of another, either through the ACQUISITION of a stake of more than 10% of a COMPANY, or by the setting up of a GREENFIELD SITE. Stakes of less than 10% are defined as PORTFOLIO investment. Many nations remain ambivalent about foreign direct investment (FDI), not wanting to see their domestic industries taken over and controlled by foreigners.

The Americans were the first to invest heavily overseas after World War II, and they were heavily criticized for it in *Le Défi Americain*, a controversial book written by a Frenchman, Jean-Jacques Servan-Schreiber. Nowadays FDI is seen more as the natural way of a global world. Many countries court it assiduously.

The Japanese have taken over from the Americans and the Europeans (particularly the Dutch and the British) as the biggest foreign direct investors around the world. If trade is the child, FDI is the adult. Japanese companies' VCR plants in Europe reduce the need to ship VCRs from plants in Japan. FDI brings nations into closer touch than long-distance trade. Japanese managers at VCR factories in Europe rub shoulders with Europeans every day. This integrates cultures in a way that nobody yet fully understands. In the future, international commercial relations are going to be shaped much more by FDI than they are by trade.

FOREIGN INVESTMENT

Investment by one country in the SECURITIES or ASSETS of another country. This includes the purchase of large chunks of industrial companies (see FOREIGN DIRECT INVESTMENT) as well as the purchase of property and of small amounts of securities.

The flows of foreign investment around the world are increasing dramatically. In one sense foreign investment is the mirror image of a CURRENT ACCOUNT surplus. If a country (like Japan) continually exports more than it imports, in its balance of payments its surplus must be "balanced" by a corresponding outflow of CAPITAL.

FORTUNE 500

The annual listing by *Fortune* of the 500 largest corporations in the United States. The magazine also publishes an annual list of the 500 largest corporations outside the United States. Companies jealously watch their positions in these rankings, the most prestigious of many. All rankings, however, suffer from a number of failings.

- It is hard to decide what measure of size to use: sales, total ASSETS, PROFIT, or MARKET capitalization (what a COMPANY is worth). All of these have been used in at least one reputable listing. (*Fortune* uses sales.)

- They all have drawbacks. For example, using sales as a yardstick always pushes to the top those companies dealing in commodity-like products (such as oil or grain). Their margins are small, and to make a reasonable business they have to have relatively huge levels of sales.

- Some yardsticks cannot cope with certain industries. Sale

figures, for instance, have little meaning for financial institutions. Banks are usually compared in terms of total assets. But total assets have little meaning for service companies, like **SOFTWARE** firms or firms of accountants. They have few assets of the type that appear on **BALANCE SHEETS**.

• By highlighting size, the listings promote the idea that big is beautiful and that size is all that matters. Companies are pushed to emphasize quantity at the expense of quality, be it of sales, profits, assets, or whatever.

FORWARD CONTRACT

A **CONTRACT** between two companies for the delivery of specified goods or currency at some specified time in the future and for a specified price. A forward contract differs from a **FUTURES** contract in that it is not entered into primarily to create a tradable instrument.

Forward contracts shift various risks from a buyer to a seller, and vice versa. For example, it considers the danger that **INFLATION** or **EXCHANGE-RATE** fluctuations will erode the **VALUE** of the contract, or that something (like a **STRIKE**) will prevent the **COMPANY** from delivering as promised.

FRANCHISE

A popular way for a manufacturer or service **COMPANY** to distribute its goods or **SERVICES** widely without making all the necessary **CAPITAL** investment itself. Some famous franchise operations include McDonald's restaurants and Benetton clothing stores.

A franchiser usually gives a license to a franchisee for a certain fee, which is frequently based on the franchisee's sales. The license gives the franchisee the exclusive right to sell the franchiser's goods or services in a particular area. In return the franchisee has to meet certain standards demanded by the franchiser (in terms of the appearance of the outlets, for example) and must buy supplies only from the franchiser. Luciano Benetton says he gives franchises not necessarily to people with merchandising experience, but to people with "the right spirit." He teaches them merchandising the Benetton way.

FRAUD

Trickery: the use of lies and deceit to obtain a material benefit. In law, CONTRACTS that are made as a result of fraud by one party can be deemed null and void by the injured party, who can subsequently claim for damages.

Fraud is as old as commercial activity itself, but it tends to thrive best in an underregulated, free-market ENVIRONMENT. Hence it was particularly prevalent in the Reaganite United States and Thatcherite United Kingdom.

Fraud is a difficult crime to prosecute, because it is often difficult to pinpoint the party who is damaged by it, as in the case of insider trading, for example. If X buys shares of COMPANY Y because he (and only he) knows that the next day company Y is going to be subject of a generous TAKEOVER bid, X clearly stands to make a big gain. But who makes a corresponding big loss?

Furthermore, it is difficult to gather the necessary evidence to bring a successful prosecution. In insider dealing, for example, it may be critical to show that a defendant knew something on a particular day (rather than on the next day). Moreover, fraud cases often involve complicated technical accounting details that judges and juries find hard to grasp.

FREE ON BOARD

A term attached to a price quotation given by an exporter. Free on board (FOB) means that the exporter undertakes, for that price, to deliver the goods to the buyer's warehouse. The French expression is *franco à bord*, and it has various modifications.

- *Franco frontier.* Free delivery to the border of the exporter's country.
- *Franco quai.* Free as far as the wharf beside the ship that is to transport the goods.
- *Franco wagon.* Free as far as the train that is to carry the goods.

FREE-TRADE ZONE

Areas where foreign goods are allowed to come and go free from TARIFFS and other barriers to trade. Often near seaports and airports, free-trade zones typically consist of a number of industrial plants where imported goods are processed before being re-exported. Since the imports never technically enter the country where the free-trade zone is located, they do not have to go through elaborate (and expensive) customs procedures. Free-trade zones are suitable for processes such as CMT (cut, make, and trim), in which imported fabric is made into garments for re-export.

Free trade, one of the greatest blessings which a government can confer on a people, is in almost every country unpopular.

Lord Macaulay

FRINGE BENEFITS

Also known as perks, these are rewards given to employees in addition to their normal wages or salaries. They include things like pensions, private health insurance, cars, sports facilities, expense accounts, low-interest loans, and (less obviously) pay for time not worked (during holidays, sickness, or TRAINING, for example). Some fringe benefits are more psychological than material, such as the addition of a name plate to a manager's door when he reaches a certain level in the corporate hierarchy.

Fringe benefits have the effect of disguising the real VALUE of an employee's remuneration. For many managers they can amount to more than 30% of salary, and they tend to tie employees more tightly to one COMPANY by creating a mini-welfare state, as it were, within the corporation.

FUTURES

CONTRACTS between parties who have different views of how things will turn out. Such contracts were first used in agricultural commodity MARKETS where a farmer might sell his produce forward (that is, before it was fully grown) to a speculator. The speculator was betting that the price of the crop would be at such a level that he could sell the produce (when he eventually took possession) at a profit. Futures markets need these two types of investor: hedgers (such as the farmer) and speculators. Hedgers play it safe; speculators take a RISK.

From agricultural commodity markets, futures spread to financial markets, first to foreign exchange, then to stocks and BONDS. Secondary markets in futures then developed to enable contracts to be bought and sold and to give LIQUIDITY to the primary market.

In futures markets the three main financial centers (corresponding to the world's three main time zones)—Tokyo in the Far East, London in Europe, and New York in the United States—have not had business all their own way. Futures markets in Singapore in the Far East, Paris in Europe, and Chicago in the United States are all providing serious COMPETITION to the traditional financial capitals.

GASTARBEITER

German for "guest worker," a migrant worker from a poor country invited to do unskilled LABOR in a rich country. *Gastarbeiter* are expected to return to their homeland after a period. They do not, therefore, have the same rights (or incur the same costs) as local employees.

GATT

See GENERAL AGREEMENT ON TARIFFS AND TRADE

GENERAL AGREEMENT ON TARIFFS AND TRADE

An international agreement signed by 22 countries when it was first drawn up in 1947, but since signed by over 100 countries, accounting for around 90% of all the world's merchandise trade. In its own words, this is the aim of the General Agreement on Tariffs and Trade (GATT):

To provide a secure and predictable international trading environment for the business community, and a continuing process of trade liberalization in which investment, job creation and trade can thrive. In this way, the multilateral trading system contributes to economic growth and development throughout the world.

The GATT attempts to persuade countries to get rid of quotas, and it acts as the secretariat for a series of multinational discussions (called "rounds") that aim to reduce TARIFFS.

The latest is called the Uruguay Round, and it is attempting to tackle areas of trade that have traditionally been excluded from the GATT's remit, such as agriculture, SERVICES, and INTELLECTUAL PROPERTY.

The GATT's main problem is that it has few teeth. When it is notified of PROTECTIONISM, there is little it can do but rely on the argument that the consequences of retaliation by others will be worse than the consequences of allowing free trade.

FRANK GILBRETH

An American building contractor who developed the ideas of FREDERICK TAYLOR, adding a psychological human element to Taylor's automatism. Gilbreth was concerned with eliminating all unnecessary motion in order to find the best way to do manual work, and he pioneered the use of the camera to help him examine human behavior. "Eliminating unnecessary distances that workers' hands and arms must travel will eliminate miles of motions per man in a working day," he wrote. In this way he improved the productivity of his bricklayers enormously.

When Gilbreth died in 1924 his wife Lilian, an industrial psychologist, took up his work and traveled the world to promote his ideas. She died in 1972 at the ripe old age of 94, having found time to give birth to 12 children.

GLASS CEILING

A phrase taken from the title of the book *Shattering the Glass Ceiling* (1988), written by Marilyn Davidson and Cary Cooper. It refers to the invisible barriers that still prevent women from climbing to the top of the MANAGEMENT ladder. In the EUROPEAN COMMUNITY as a whole, women make up almost 40% of the workforce. Yet less than 2% of top managers are women. Even in Scandinavia, where equal opportunities are widely assumed to be greatest, less than 10% of all management jobs are filled by women.

With the LABOR shortage that the demographic squeeze will bring to much of Europe, countries need to look at ways in which they can make better managerial use of this underdeveloped two-fifths of their workforce.

Common reasons cited for the glass ceiling include the following:

The pipeline. Senior managers take 20 to 25 years to reach the top level of their careers. Women have not been managers in significant numbers for that long; in other words they are in the pipeline, but they have not yet emerged at the top.

Lack of broad-based experience. Women tend to choose (and be chosen for) jobs in support SERVICES. They get little opportunity to work in line management. This has given rise to the phrase "the glass elevator"; even women who do rise to the top do so from within narrow specializations, typically in HUMAN RESOURCES or communications.

The family. Even in two-career families where the woman has pursued an independent career and had children, it is usually the woman who gives up a career should the pressures become intolerable. During their main childbearing years, between 25 and 34, women's job aspirations decline dramatically.

A hostile corporate ENVIRONMENT. As a general rule, like will promote like. In other words, a boss will choose someone like himself to replace him (and why not, since he was so perfect for the job?). Since most bosses are men, they tend to replace themselves with men.

The rules of the game were made by men. Women cannot rewrite them, so they have to demonstrate both male and female attributes, a tall order.

GLOBAL BRAND

That elite group of products whose brand name is recognized across the globe; Levi's, Coca-Cola, McDonald's, and Nescafé, for example. Americans seem particularly good at creating global brands for popular products, Europeans less so. However, Europeans have been very successful at creating global brands for luxury goods: for example, in cars (Porsche, Mercedes, Rolls-Royce, and so on), in drinks (cognacs, champagnes, whiskies), and in fashion (Armani, Saint Laurent, and so on).

The Japanese have been less concerned with branding. With the notable exception of the Walkman, Japanese brand names fail to register with anything like the strength of U.S. and European brands. Their greatest brand name is now Japan itself.

GLOBAL VILLAGE

The idea that **INFORMATION TECHNOLOGY** and fast air travel have brought the world closer together, giving the whole globe some of the qualities of a village. This is hardly surprising since it now takes less time to travel from London to New York than it took Wordsworth in his Lakeland village to reach the nearest mailbox.

IT and fast air travel have developed a number of global villages. They are not geographically distinct; their inhabitants are drawn to each other by a common interest or purpose rather than by physical proximity. Thus currency dealers or stockbrokers in London, New York, and Tokyo probably talk to each other more often and understand each other better than do their neighbors in the suburbs where they live.

GOING CONCERN

A key concept in accounting, where auditors base many of their valuations for the purposes of a **COMPANY'S** accounts on the assumption that the business is going to continue for a while (as a "going concern"). If it is not likely to continue, the value of its stock and of plant and machinery, for example, is very different. As a going concern, plant is a productive asset, and stock can be expected to be sold at or above full **COST**. In a company about to go bust, plant and machinery may be only good for scrap, and stock no more valuable than items in a clearance sale.

GOING PRIVATE

The transformation of a **PUBLIC COMPANY** into a private company, the opposite of **GOING PUBLIC**.

GOING PUBLIC

The process of transforming a private COMPANY owned by a few shareholders into a PUBLIC COMPANY whose SHARES can be traded among members of the public, and whose share price is quoted on a stock exchange. Going public can be expensive, requiring the services of an investment bank (to prepare the documentation) plus considerable legal and accounting fees.

Going public is the pot of gold at the end of the rainbow for most ENTREPRENEURS. It enables them to sell some of their shares and thereby to cash in on their creation.

GOLDEN HANDCUFFS

A form of reward given to key employees that ties them to the COMPANY and/or (perhaps just as importantly) prevents them from working for a rival. Golden handcuffs come in several shapes, each with its own degree of gilt, for example:

- A cheap, long-term loan that the employer knows the employee will have difficulty paying back at short notice
- A lump-sum payment in return for a contractual obligation not to work for a rival for a stated period of time

Golden handcuffs extend more widely than is generally appreciated. Any employee with a pension or a company car is handcuffed by the inconvenience (and expense) of buying a new car and/or changing pension programs.

GOLDEN PARACHUTE

An expression coined in the 1980s to describe the employment CONTRACTS that top managers wrote for themselves when they felt that their COMPANY might be subject to a TAKEOVER and that they might be out of a job. The contracts stipulated that should such a situation occur, the managers would receive huge compensation on their dismissal. In some cases the compensation was to be paid even if the managers were merely pushed to one side, and not actually dismissed.

Such abuses of MANAGEMENT'S power should, of course, be checked by shareholders. But they often see golden parachutes as a deterrent to takeovers which they themselves may not relish.

GOODWILL

The amount that an acquiring COMPANY A pays for another company B over and above the VALUE of B's ASSETS. Goodwill is thus the amount paid for the fact that there is more to B than meets an accountant's eye, including:

- the goodwill (in the literal sense) of its customers
- the value of its brands
- the value of its unfinished RESEARCH AND DEVELOPMENT
- the value of its MANAGEMENT team

None of these elements appears in the annual financial statements. After an ACQUISITION this intangible "goodwill" has to be dealt with in the accounts of the merged company. It is usually deducted from PROFITS gradually over a number of years.

GREENFIELD SITE

A site for a new FACTORY or office that has hitherto been unused for industrial or commercial purposes.

GUARANTEE

There are four main commercial meanings.

1. A promise given by a manufacturer that an article sold is of a certain quality. If the article is found to be faulty within a specified period, the manufacturer guarantees to repair or replace it.

2. A promise by a third party to pay a debt should certain conditions not be fulfilled by the parties to the debt CONTRACT. This is helpful, for example, when new companies

are trying to raise a loan; the directors give personal guarantees. If the COMPANY does not repay the loan, then they do.

3. A bank guarantee is a written promise from a bank to repay a debt to a third party if the DEBTOR does not do so by a certain date.

4. A PERFORMANCE guarantee is an amount (normally 5–10% of the VALUE of a contract) that a customer withholds from a supplier until the contract is completely fulfilled.

Halo effect

The phenomenon whereby a complex set of stimuli is judged on the basis of only one of them, the one whose "halo" outshines all the rest.

This is important in at least two areas of business.

Interviewing potential employees. People are able to totally ignore major character defects because (for example) a candidate is smartly dressed.

Buying products. Consumers will often overlook obvious deficiencies in the product because the manufacturer is, say, kind to trees.

Hard sell

A MARKETING term to describe very aggressive ways of selling products or SERVICES. Certain industries are renowned for their hard-sell methods: time sharing (for vacations), life insurance, and everything about Christmas, for example.

Hard sell is the opposite of soft sell, a marketing technique so subtle that its effect is almost subliminal. A soft sell involves the use of images and design to associate a product with a particular lifestyle or pleasurable situation (like falling in love).

Hardware

The pots and pans of the COMPUTER world, the computer equipment that you can kick: the monitor, the keyboard, the DISK DRIVE, and the printer. The opposite of SOFTWARE.

Hard work never killed anybody. But worrying about it did.

Anon

Hawthorne effect

This is the most famous finding of what is probably the most well-known industrial experiment of all time. The experiment started in 1927 at the General Electric Company's Hawthorne factory in Chicago and continued for a decade or so thereafter. Involving some 20,000 workers and almost 100 investigators from Harvard, it was led by an Australian social psychologist called Elton Mayo.

The Hawthorne effect was the discovery that factory workers worked harder when the level of lighting in their plant was increased. They worked harder again when the lighting intensity decreased. It was not the physical conditions per se that were motivating them, but the knowledge that somebody somewhere was concerned about their physical welfare.

Headhunter

A person who specializes in finding and recruiting senior managers and professional staff on behalf of others. This can be very lucrative as headhunters often receive in commission up to one-third of the first-year's salary of those whom they place. They do well in industries where particular skills are in short supply—for example, in the finance industry on Wall Street. Sometimes they recruit whole teams of financial specialists, tempting them from one firm and persuading them to join another. Headhunting agencies are also known as executive search firms.

Head office

For top managers, a clubhouse; for the rest, an excuse for inaction, as in: "I'll have to ask head office." One of industry's most significant discoveries in the 1980s was that it did not need the huge head offices favored in the 1960s and 1970s. These grandiose buildings contained two types of workers, both of whom became increasingly redundant.

Corporate planners. These people could spend weeks transcribing the minutiae of a COMPANY'S future plans. As the pace of change increased, the need for this precision diminished. Long-term plans were out of date the day after they were written.

Information pushers. These people channeled information from the top of the corporation downward and outward. Less frequently they pushed it in the opposite direction. COMPUTERS and INFORMATION TECHNOLOGY took over their function far more efficiently.

HEAVY INDUSTRY

Any manufacturer who makes big things (like ships) with big machines and weighty RAW MATERIALS. "Heavy" sounds serious, as opposed to its opposite—"light industry"—which sounds frivolous, but it is light industry that keeps the Western world wealthy. Heavy industry is increasingly being dispersed to developing countries.

HIERARCHY

There are two meanings.

1. The order of importance of different jobs within an organization. Traditionally, companies have placed great weight on hierarchy, as have the military from whom such concepts were borrowed. However, hierarchy-conscious companies breed hierarchy-conscious employees, and hence rigidity. In the more flexible workplace of the future, both employer and employee will largely have to live without the social road map that hierarchy provides. Hierarchy is important to those who believe in THEORY X, but not to those who believe in THEORY Y.

2. The psychological "hierarchy of needs" that is at the core of ABRAHAM MASLOW'S widely respected work on motivation.

High tech

Something that is technologically advanced: "The COMPANY is moving into high-tech businesses like body scanners and color photocopiers." There is an impression that high tech is good and low tech is bad. Yet some of the most profitable businesses are in low-tech industries.

As with HEAVY INDUSTRY, high tech demonstrates how the choice of language in business influences the way we think of business. High tech sounds modern; low tech sounds base. The reality is very different.

Historic cost

The starting point for almost all accounting calculations: the COST of a COMPANY'S ASSETS when it was originally purchased. Accountants like this because it is a real amount of money that was once actually paid by somebody, unlike some other costs that are mere theoretical calculations.

The trouble with historic cost is that it takes no note of the passage of time. DEPRECIATION is the technique that accountants use to take account of the effects of wear and tear on a company's assets, and of the fact that companies need to put aside money to replace an asset as and when it is worn out. The cost of replacing an asset that was bought five years ago may be more or less than it was then. It will certainly not be the same.

Human resources

The modern term for LABOR, one of the three factors of production along with CAPITAL and RAW MATERIALS. In recent decades industry has gone through cycles in which it has put undue emphasis on one of these factors or another.

The 1970s was the decade of raw materials, with OPEC (OR-GANIZATION OF PETROLEUM EXPORTING COUNTRIES) successfully monopolizing the oil MARKET, a frenzy of excitement about rather useless commodities like gold and silver, and the setting up of a number of COMMODITY AGREEMENTS that soon proved unworkable.

The 1980s was the decade of capital, with investment bankers throwing money at projects that number-wise accountants told them were sure to make a PROFIT. In too many cases they were wrong.

The 1990s looks prepared to be the decade of human resources, when companies get terribly concerned about training their workforce and about holding on to a decreasing number of highly trained employees. As in previous decades the enthusiasm will probably be overdone.

HURDLE RATE

A RATE OF RETURN crucial in making judgments about CAPITAL expenditure. The hurdle rate is that rate of return required for the project to be worthwhile, that is, a higher rate of return than would have been obtained by leaving the capital idle in a bank. The project's expected rate of return is calculated by using DISCOUNTED CASH FLOW techniques.

IMF

See **INTERNATIONAL MONETARY FUND**

IMPORT QUOTA

A form of **PROTECTIONISM** in which a country sets a limit (a quota) on the quantity (or weight) of certain goods that it will allow to be imported across its borders. Import quotas can be very precisely targeted at a specific exporting country, product, or time, and are thus a useful weapon in a trade war. They can often be circumvented, however, by passing the goods through a third country.

INCENTIVE

Anything that encourages an employee to work harder and to be more productive. An "incentive **BONUS**" is a bonus paid for production that is in excess of an agreed amount. This is a variation on the **PIECE-RATE** system.

INDIRECT COST

A **COST** that cannot be directly attributed to a particular product. Such costs include the wages of employees who work on the manufacture of several products (general managers or supervisors, for example), and the cost of machines that are used in the manufacture of more than one product. These costs have to be allocated to each product in one way or another in order to calculate the price at which the product is to be sold profitably.

INDUSTRIAL ACTION

See **STRIKE**

INDUSTRIAL ESPIONAGE

Spying on companies to obtain secrets for somebody else's commercial benefit. In most countries the law is remarkably unclear about whether it is illegal to steal trade secrets or not. In one case an industrial spy was jailed for stealing paper from his employer, not for stealing the sensitive company information that was on the paper.

When secrets disappear across a border, it is even more difficult to obtain legal redress. The absence of adequate PATENTS and recognition of INTELLECTUAL PROPERTY rights in many countries mean that the international theft of ideas is big business, particularly in the pharmaceutical and COMPUTER industries.

There have been several major cases involving the theft by Japanese companies of computer-industry secrets from U.S. firms. During the cold war East Germany was reckoned to have had more industrial than political spies in West Germany. Their intelligence saved East Germany billions of dollars a year.

INDUSTRIAL POLICY

The nature and extent of government intervention in a nation's industry, this varies greatly from country to country. Most countries have a policy of encouraging investment in industry, and they set about it armed with a host of investment grants and tax incentives.

For some, industrial policy is no more than a part of regional policy (trying to encourage industry to set up in particularly depressed areas) or of environmental policy (giving grants to firms to cut down on their emission of noxious gases, for example).

A few believe that it should be no more than competition policy. In the free-wheeling Anglo-Saxon world of the 1980s, industrial policy extended little further than a government department to ensure that competition was both free and fair.

Encouraging investment was done by lowering tax rates so that individuals could save (and invest) for themselves.

INDUSTRIAL PSYCHOLOGY

The study of human behavior in a working environment. This is a favorite area of study for MANAGEMENT academics whose work has focused on a number of areas.

LEADERSHIP. What does it take to be a COMPANY boss? Can the skills be learned? Can potential leaders be identified at an early stage?

MOTIVATION. What makes workers more productive, the fact that soft factors (like feeling needed) are as important as hard factors, like pay and FRINGE BENEFITS.

Team building. How to make groups work better together, a skill the Japanese have developed to a high degree.

INDUSTRIAL RELATIONS

A subject that has a more narrow meaning than its name implies. It does not cover the whole range of relations in industry—between supplier and manufacturer, manufacturer and customer, and so on—but only the narrow subject of relations between employers, TRADE UNIONS, and the government departments that watch over them. The state of industrial relations in a nation can be measured roughly by the number of working days lost through STRIKES.

INDUSTRIAL REVOLUTION

The process of social and economic change whereby an agricultural country turns into a manufacturing one: farmers head for the cities and jobs in newly opened factories. The first industrial revolution occurred in the United Kingdom at the end of the eighteenth and the beginning of the nineteenth centuries. Behind it were new ideas about MASS PRODUCTION and the division of LABOR, and it was propelled by a spate of scientific inventions that came with the almost simultaneous discovery of steam and coal power.

INFLATION

The economic phenomenon of a general rise in prices. The most commonly used measure of inflation is the increase in the price of a "basket" of retail goods over a period of time. Very rarely in history have nations experienced a negative rate of inflation (that is an across-the-board fall in prices).

Some degree of inflation is generally accepted as inevitable. A very high rate is undesirable because of the uncertainty it creates and because it hurts creditors (to the benefit of debtors) and those on fixed incomes.

One of the main causes of inflation is high growth in an economy's money supply, that is, sending out more notes and coins to chase a fixed amount of goods. The result is that the price of those goods rises.

When I first started working I used to dream of the day I might be earning the salary I'm now starving on.

Saying to show evils of inflation

INFORMATION TECHNOLOGY

The combination of COMPUTERS and telecommunications, and the remarkable things that they can achieve together. It is sometimes known as informatics and more commonly as its abbreviation, IT.

IT has changed the way in which companies organize themselves. By making information instantly available to almost anybody anywhere, it has reduced the need for the middle manager who just pushed paper from the top of the organization to the bottom.

In turn, lower levels of employees now receive more information, demanding a higher degree of skill and judgment on their part. Information technology has also encouraged companies to go into new geographical markets, secure in the knowledge that with IT they can keep a proper eye on the business.

Nothing is worse for morale than a lack of information down in the ranks. I call it NETMA—nobody ever tells me anything—and I have tried to minimize that problem.

Ed Carlson, when president of United Airlines

INNOVATION

Francis Bacon, the Elizabethan poet, was as interested in the process of innovation as any of today's MANAGEMENT gurus:

He that will not apply new remedies must expect new evils; for time is the greatest innovator.

Truly excellent companies—like 3M, inventor of Post-it note pads and Scotch Tape—focus strongly on innovation. At 3M it is seen as a perpetual process, driven by technology. The COMPANY has a specific objective of ensuring that at least 25% of its turnover comes from products that have been in existence for less than five years. 3M employees are allowed to spend up to 15% of their working hours doing anything they want, as long as it is related to the company's products.

Innovation is a critical part of the business process: the addition of new elements to products or SERVICES, or to the methods of producing them. Innovation is not the creation of an entirely new product; that is invention, and it is relatively rare. It is, rather, the continuous process of adding to and improving a product in order to gain an edge over its competitors. This can only be done by listening closely to customers. Almost all IBM's early innovations came from collaboration with its leading customer, the Census Office.

Lowell Steele, for many years the manager responsible for innovation at General Electric, wrote an article for the *Harvard Business Review* in 1983 in which he listed seven popular misconceptions about technology.

1. The best technology possible should always be implemented.
2. What is "good enough" is always determined rationally.
3. Most innovations are successful.
4. MURPHY'S LAW does not apply to technical innovation.
5. The more original the idea, the better.
6. Technical success is the major hurdle that an innovation has to cross.
7. Routines, standards, and similar constraints are not important in technology development.

Remember that Steele maintained that all seven of the above were *wrong*.

Innovation comes from creative destruction.

Yoshihisa Tabuchi, president, Nomura Securities

After 29 years of experience in nurturing innovation at General Electric, I am still amazed by how fragile and improbable a process innovation really is.

Lowell Steele, senior manager, General Electric

Innovation is 1% inspiration and 99% perspiration.

Thomas Edison

Business is not the art of having new ideas all the time. It is the art of using your new ideas sparingly, and in the right dosage, at the right moment.

Georges Doriot, Harvard Business School

INSOLVENCY

The condition of a COMPANY that is unable to repay its debts as and when they become due. Insolvency is not necessarily fatal. Companies can attempt to reschedule their debts, either informally with their creditors or formally through legal processes like CHAPTER 11.

INTANGIBLE ASSETS

ASSETS that cannot be kicked. An accounting term used to refer to things like GOODWILL, PATENTS, brand names, and TRADEMARKS, which have a VALUE even though they are (literally) intangible. While nobody denies that these things are worth something, problems arise when they try to decide how much.

INTELLECTUAL PROPERTY

Ideas, inventions, designs, or books that belong to their creator. Although intellectual property can be protected by PATENT, registered TRADEMARK, and COPYRIGHT, it is particularly vulnerable to theft.

Intellectual property is set to be the next most contentious area of international trade. The International Trade Commission estimates that U.S. companies alone lose $40 billion to $50 billion a year (almost half the nation's trade deficit) from the unauthorized use of American technology by foreign manufacturers.

In a landmark judgment in a New Jersey court in 1992, Honeywell was awarded $96 million compensation for technology stolen by the Japanese camera company Minolta. From 1984 Honeywell inventions had been used by Minolta in its autofocus and automatic lens shutter cameras, and not a yen was paid to Honeywell in royalties.

As a result of its experience, Honeywell believes that certain international rules are needed to protect intellectual property.

- Common standards for patents, trademarks, and copyrights
- A compatible international patent system
- Mechanisms for a timely resolution of disputes (most logically within the GATT)
- Rigorous enforcement rules, including border controls

INTEREST COVER

The number of times that a business can pay its interest out of its pre-tax **PROFITS**. (Banks watch this figure keenly.) Likewise, **DIVIDEND** cover is the number of times that a **COMPANY'S** dividends can be paid out of its pre-tax profits.

INTERFACE

The **HARDWARE** and **SOFTWARE** that lie between two **COMPUTERS**, allowing them to communicate with each other. From this rather specialist technical meaning, the word is now used (pretentiously) in many business contexts: "He had great difficulty interfacing with his colleagues from New York," or "The design process sits at the interface between production and consumption."

INTERNAL RATE OF RETURN

The internal rate of return (IRR) is the interest rate at which the discounted future **CASH FLOW** from a project exactly equals the investment in the project. In general, this must be higher than the marginal cost of **CAPITAL** for it to be worth proceeding with the project.

INTERNATIONAL LABOR ORGANIZATION

The International Labor Organization (ILO) is an agency of the United Nations based in Geneva. Originally set up in 1919 under the Treaty of Versailles, its purpose is to encourage the introduction of good LABOR laws and to improve working conditions all over the world. It has more than 100 member countries, each of which is represented by two government officials plus one representative each for employers and employees. The ILO is an invaluable source of international statistics.

INTERNATIONAL MONETARY FUND

The International Monetary Fund (IMF) was set up to police the Bretton Woods Agreement, an international treaty signed in 1944 by the world's major nations, pledging to maintain fixed exchange rates between their currencies. The IMF has the power to lend considerable sums to member countries, based on the size of their "quota," that is, the membership subscriptions they pay, which are roughly related to the size of their economies.

The IMF's principal function largely disappeared once fixed exchange rates were abandoned in the early 1970s. It found a new role for itself by becoming more involved with member countries' economic policies, and in particular with those of heavily indebted countries (for example, Brazil and Mexico) caught up in the international debt crisis of the early 1980s. With the break-up of Comecon in Eastern Europe, the IMF has found itself another significant role in overseeing the economic transformation from communism to capitalism of countries in the region.

INTERPERSONAL SKILLS

A long term for the ability of people to get on well together. Interpersonal skills can be developed quite methodically for use in formal situations such as interviewing or negotiating (for example, do not fold your arms during a NEGOTIATION because it looks defensive).

Many people also believe such skills can be developed to help them "win friends and influence people." At least as many believe that they cannot.

In the academic world there is a discipline devoted to the study of interpersonal relationships. To my knowledge, however, not one scholar specializes in the study of intercompany relationships.

Kenichi Ohmae

INTERVIEW

It is important to structure an interview for a job in a way that will get the best out of the candidates and also ensure that the best person for the job is selected.

Here are the sorts of questions to ask in an interview:

Open questions. To encourage the interviewee to talk, for example: "Why does this position interest you?"

Closed questions. Requiring a yes or no answer: "Do you always meet your deadlines?"

Specific questions. Asking for specific information, such as: "Which COMPUTER systems have you used?"

Reflective questions. Considering remarks already made during the interview and connecting them to an area you are currently discussing, for instance: "You mentioned earlier . . ." or "Can you explain . . ."

Hypothetical questions. To show the candidate's speed of thought and creativity, for example: "If you hadn't taken your last job, what do you think you might be doing now?"

INTRAPRENEURSHIP

A neologism that combines the idea of entrepreneurship with intra (the Latin for inside or within). It is the promotion of the qualities of the ENTREPRENEUR inside a big corporation. Intrapreneurship became popular in the 1980s with the realization that small entrepreneurial firms were nimble and quick to change, while large companies were like dinosaurs, in danger of extinction because their brains were too small for their bodies.

IRR

See INTERNAL RATE OF RETURN

IT

See INFORMATION TECHNOLOGY

JIT

See **JUST-IN-TIME**

JOBBING

A system of production used when the quantity of goods to be produced is too small to justify either **BATCH** production or **MASS PRODUCTION**. Jobbing is often found in the engineering industry where orders (for machine tools, for instance) are in very small numbers. Such production needs particularly careful planning, each product requiring different operations in a different sequence. With jobbing it is very difficult to forecast production times.

JOINT VENTURE

A business venture entered into jointly by two or more partners. Companies favor joint ventures when they are exploring a new **MARKET** or a new geographical region. Their main aim is to share the **RISK**, but it helps if one of the partners has some local or specialized knowledge of the market to be explored. Joint ventures have become popular as more companies have looked to new markets abroad.

Many joint ventures split up after a while, with the partners deciding to go their own separate ways. Although these splits are often acrimonious, they do not mean that the joint venture was a failure. It may just be a natural stage in this way of starting a business.

Some joint ventures have a long and impressive track record: Unilever, the Anglo-Dutch giant, is the result of a joint venture between the United Kingdom's Lever Brothers and the Netherlands' J. Van den Bergh. It is now far bigger than either of its founders.

JUNK BOND

The emotionally charged name for a certain sort of debt security popular in the 1980s. Forever associated with the now-defunct investment bank Drexel Burnham Lambert and with its criminal chief junk-bond dealer Michael Milken, junk bonds have come to smell worse than junk.

Their image is not entirely fair. Technically a junk bond is no more than a bond issued by an organization in the United States that has less than a certain rating from the main credit-rating agencies; in 1985 it was a rating below BAA from Moody's or below BBB from Standard & Poor's. Many U.S. pension funds and insurance companies are strictly limited in the number of bonds that they can buy with a "junk" rating.

In the mid-1980s fewer than 1,000 companies merited higher than a junk rating. That left some 20,000 U.S. companies with ASSETS of more than $25 million and virtually no access to the bond MARKET, until Drexel came along and created a market for them.

Drexel's great success was in persuading investors that the extra reward on these high-yielding bonds considerably outweighed the extra RISK. That was true for as long as junk was issued by basically sound small companies from the heartlands. But as recession began to bite, once glamour-rated companies set off on a steeply declining ratings curve, ripping through BBB on their way to BANKRUPTCY. They were genuinely junk, and they temporarily killed the market for others who were not.

JUST-IN-TIME

A technique of stock CONTROL that aims to minimize the amount of stocks that a manufacturing COMPANY has to hold. Developed in the 1960s by the Toyota car company in Japan, just-in-time (JIT) has come to assume magical powers as one of the techniques that contributed most to the Japanese industrial miracle.

The core of the idea is quite simple: each stage in the production process calls for parts as and when it needs them. This can result in one unit receiving as many as 10 deliveries a day. The system also breaks down the ASSEMBLY-LINE operation into small units, each of which is responsible for delivery to another similarly small unit.

KAISHA

The great Japanese corporations that have grown up since World War II and have been the major source of Japan's economic strength. Celebrated in an illuminating book of the same name—*Kaisha, the Japanese Corporation*, by James C. Abegglen and George Stalk—Kaisha such as Honda, Toyota, and Canon have developed unique **MANAGEMENT** systems and qualities that, argue Abegglen and Stalk, have great virtues, but also some weaknesses.

> *The best of the kaisha are creative, flexible, and powerful competitors. However, it is also true that at their worst, many of the kaisha are slow to react, with underutilized assets, poorly rewarded employees and shareholders, aging facilities, and undistinguished management . . . the range of competence among Japan's companies should not be overlooked.*

Abegglen and Stalk should know what they are talking about. They both spent many years in the Tokyo office of The Boston Consulting Group, creator of the **BOSTON MATRIX**.

KANBAN

The cards that constitute orders for parts in the famous **JUST-IN-TIME** (JIT) production system devised by Japan's Toyota motor company. When a team working on one part of the Toyota manufacturing process needs parts from another team, it merely sends the empty parts tray together with the tray's kanban. This constitutes a production order to the second team. The demand for parts thus filters backwards through the manufacturing process.

KEIRETSU

See **ZAIBATSU**

JOHN MAYNARD KEYNES

Arguably the most influential economist of the twentieth century, also associated with a famous literary group (the Bloomsbury Group) that revolved around Virginia Woolf and her sister Vanessa Bell.

Keynes's most famous book, *General Theory of Employment, Interest and Money,* was published in 1936 at the depth of the depression. Its main message was that countries' economies could get stuck in a statistically healthy-looking equilibrium at the same time that they had massive unemployment. It was governments' responsibility to stimulate demand and create full employment.

Governments learned the lesson, but by the 1970s they were being accused of creating not only extra demand, but INFLATION too. Economists then turned their attention to the trade-off between inflation and unemployment.

> *We are all Keynesians now.*
>
> Richard Nixon in 1971

KICKBACK

An illegal payment made in specific circumstances, in particular, by an employee to an employer who has agreed (with unions or government) to pay a certain MINIMUM WAGE. In order to get the job at all, the employee agrees to pay a percentage of his or her salary to the employer.

A kickback can also be a payment to a government official from a supplier for his or her help in obtaining a particular PUBLIC-SECTOR CONTRACT. Since such contracts are often huge, the temptation for both the briber and the bribed can be very strong. (See PUBLIC PROCUREMENT)

KNOW-HOW

A salable technique or skill that has been developed by a COMPANY. For example, when JIT was first developed it was known as the Toyota manufacturing system. For a while, until other companies adopted the idea, JIT was a part of Toyota's know-how.

Know-how may be more tangibly attributed to products: the recipe for Sara Lee's Pecan Pie, for example, or the technique of semifreezing prepared foods developed by Marks & Spencer. Once it is widely available and widely used, however, its VALUE diminishes. When everybody knows how, there is no know-how.

Facts are power.

Harold Geneen, CEO, ITT

KNOWLEDGE-WORKER

A neologism for a worker whose job depends on having access to knowledge about the corporation, knowledge that is disseminated by INFORMATION TECHNOLOGY. Typically, knowledge-workers include airline sales staff or car-rental staff, people who cannot do their job (selling tickets or allocating cars) without COMPUTERS to inform them of what is available.

Knowledge-workers are contrasted with old-style manual workers who learned one skill and then repeated it again and again without any change in their work ENVIRONMENT or any requirement for further information. Knowledge-workers are constantly "interfacing" with their employers.

Labor

Human work, and one of the economists' three so-called factors of production: land, labor, and CAPITAL (see also FACTORY). Economists call the price of labor "wages."

The price of a manager, of course, is a salary and a bunch of perks (see FRINGE BENEFITS). Managers do not like to think that what they do is labor, but they use the word in a number of contexts.

Casual labor. Workers, particularly in the construction industry, who work on and off, as and when needed.

Labor-intensive. The sort of product or service that requires a high input of labor for every unit produced and is therefore appropriately produced in a country with ample spare labor (see CAPITAL-INTENSIVE).

Labor mobility. The willingness of workers to relocate as necessary in order to start a new job.

Labor relations. (See INDUSTRIAL RELATIONS)

LAN

See LOCAL AREA NETWORK

Laptop

A type of COMPUTER that can be used on the lap, particularly useful for business trips by train or plane, where there is a lot of spare time but not a lot of spare room.

A laptop computer is scarcely distinguishable from a "portable computer." The main difference is that some portable computers require a source of electricity. The essential feature of the laptop is that it can be run for a reasonable length of time on rechargeable batteries. The smallest laptops are often called notebook computers.

LAST IN, FIRST OUT

Commonly known by its acronym LIFO, it is the opposite of FIFO
(FIRST IN, FIRST OUT). It is the method of accounting for stocks
that assumes that the last stocks to be purchased are the first
to be used in production.

The later the stocks are bought, the more expensive they are.
So LIFO effectively increases a COMPANY'S costs. Hence under
LIFO companies have lower profits than under FIFO.

---

*Any survey of what businessmen are reading
runs smack into the open secret that
most businessmen aren't.*

Marilyn Bender

LEADERSHIP

An indefinable quality that makes some people good at activat-
ing others in a particular direction. That direction is not always
benign: Attila the Hun, Napoleon, and Hitler were all great leaders. So, arguably, were Al Capone and Robert Maxwell.

There are some basic traits that are supposed to mark those
people who have the quality of leadership, such as VISION, integ-
rity, and a willingness to take RISKS. Leaders are also persistent
and will try anything to achieve their goals. They lead by in-
stinct. Managers who are out of touch with their instincts are
never going to make good leaders. Some researchers believe that
leaders are also more likely to have been the eldest or only child
in their family, inner-directed rather than responsive to others.

Warren Bennis, one of the most widely read gurus on leadership, goes along with the inner-directed view, developing an
idea put forward by David Riesman in a 1950s book called *The
Lonely Crowd*. In his book *On Becoming a Leader* (1989),

Bennis examined 28 subjects who he maintained were true leaders. He found that a surprisingly high number of them had had multiple careers, and they themselves believed that the multiplicity had helped them to become leaders. The typical leader is not a person who has spent 30 years climbing the ladder of the same organization.

Companies and business schools spend an enormous amount of time trying to distill the essence of leadership. Here is one attempt from Abraham Zaleznik, a respected academic in the field, who believes that natural leaders have the following characteristics:

- They are active rather than reactive, shaping ideas rather than responding to them.
- They take a personal and active attitude toward goals and ambitions.
- They develop quite fresh ways of looking at old problems.
- They are more interested in what events mean to others than in their own role in getting things accomplished.
- They are often viewed with strong emotion by others.
- They tend to feel somewhat apart from their ENVIRONMENT and from other people.

Masao Nemoto, a managing director of Toyota, Japan's biggest car company, pioneered many of the practices of TOTAL QUALITY MANAGEMENT and of JUST-IN-TIME (JIT) production that are now commonplace in manufacturing industries around the world. Nemoto also enunciated his 10 "principles of leadership":

1. Continually look for ways to improve the performance of employees.
2. Coordinate work between different divisions.
3. Everyone should have the opportunity to speak in meetings of QUALITY CIRCLES and at other MANAGEMENT/worker meetings.

4. Do not scold. If you shoot the messenger he will never report back on problems with systems or strategies.

5. Make sure others understand your work.

6. Send the best employees out for training. Do not keep them tied to the factory floor in the belief that you cannot manage without them.

7. A command without a deadline is not a command.

8. Rehearsal (of presentations, for example) is an ideal time for training, particularly in presentation skills (which Toyota values highly).

9. Top management must take action whenever a problem is identified. Delegating responsibility is ineffective.

10. Ask subordinates, "What can I do for you?" At Toyota this is known as "creating an opportunity to be heard at the top."

One of the most important functions of a division manager is to improve coordination between his own division and other divisions. If you cannot handle this task, please go to work for an American company.

Masao Nemoto, managing director of Toyota, to the car company's employees

---

LEADING AND LAGGING

Indicators of the economic activity of a nation are either leading indicators—they come before the economic event they are FORE-CASTING, or lagging indicators—coming after an economic change that they can confirm. The United States puts a number of leading indicators together into a closely watched "leading indicators index."

LEAD TIME

The time between placing an order for something and receiving it. Lead times are an important variable in the planning of production processes.

LEARNING CURVE

The graph of knowledge over time, a slope that (normally) moves from the bottom left-hand corner to the top right-hand corner, with time measured along the horizontal axis. "He's on a steep learning curve" refers to someone who has to pick up new skills quickly.

LEARNING ORGANIZATION

A concept developed by the behavioral psychologist Chris Argyris that describes the COMPANY (or organization) that "learns" as its employees learn. In the learning organization, systems and methods are altered to take advantage of things learned. In that way the organization retains knowledge independent of its employees.

LEASING

The hiring of expensive ASSETS, like machinery, by a manufacturer from a financial COMPANY. This is obviously useful for manufacturers who cannot afford to pay the full COST of the assets. It is also (less obviously) a clever scheme to benefit fully from tax allowances. Manufacturers often pay too little tax to enable them to take advantage of all the allowances on their purchase of CAPITAL goods. Finance companies pay plenty of tax against which to set capital allowances. Put the two together, share the allowances, and you have leasing.

"Lease-back" refers to the practice whereby a company sells a building that it owns to a property or finance company and immediately leases it back. This releases cash that the company can use for other purposes.

LETTER OF CREDIT

An arrangement with a bank to obtain payment, usually abroad. A bank writes a letter to another bank in which it gives the right to a third party to withdraw money up to a stated amount, an amount for which the writer of the letter takes responsibility.

It sounds complicated, but it is not. The first bank is usually writing the letter on behalf of a customer (whose account is debited with the amount in question). This customer is buying something from the customer of the second bank who wants to be sure of getting the money before the goods are shipped.

There are a number of different types of letters of credit (L/C).

Confirmed L/C. This carries a promise from the vendor's bank that it will be responsible for any credit given to its customer.

Documentary L/C. This is an L/C to which the vendor has to attach a number of documents (such as a BILL OF LADING or a consular seal) before being paid.

Irrevocable L/C. This is an L/C that cannot be revoked without the permission of the person to whom the payment is being made.

LETTER OF INTENT

A written declaration that the writer intends to follow a particular course of action (such as buying another COMPANY) if certain things happen, for example, if the company's books are as they say they are when the writer examines them. A letter of intent is not a legally binding promise. It is little better than the word of the person who writes it.

KURT LEWIN

A German professor of psychology at Berlin University who emigrated to the United States in 1932. There he founded the Center for Group Dynamics and was influential in the thinking behind London's Tavistock Institute. He believed that behavior patterns needed to be "unfrozen" before new ones could be learned and frozen in their place. To do this Lewin designed the **T-GROUP**, which encouraged people to gather together in teams for a little painful soul-searching on the way to more effective group behavior.

LIABILITIES

Things on the opposite side of a **BALANCE SHEET** to **ASSETS**: what is owed by a business to its creditors. A **COMPANY'S** assets minus its liabilities equal its **NET WORTH**, the underlying **VALUE** belonging to its shareholders.

LICENSING

The granting to somebody of a right that would otherwise be illegal for them to exercise. For example, a pharmaceutical **COMPANY** may give somebody a license to sell in a foreign **MARKET** a drug that is still produced by **PATENT**.

LIFO

See **LAST IN, FIRST OUT**

RENSIS LIKERT

A psychologist who developed an influential concept of **MANAGEMENT** styles while working for the Institute for Social Research at the University of Michigan.

1. The authoritarian manager, who believes in coercing people to do as they are told.

2. The benevolent authoritarian type, who uses a carrot rather than a stick to get people to do as they are told.

3. The consultative manager, who talks things through with junior colleagues even though she makes the decisions in the end.

4. The participative type, who encourages subordinates to make decisions together and then watches over them to ensure that they achieve their targets.

The second style, Likert maintained, is the most common, but the last is the most effective in the long term.

Limited liability

One of the great inventions of capitalism, the granting to a COMPANY by law of a limit to its liability. For a company limited by SHARES, the maximum liability is the share capital, effectively the amount still unpaid on the shares (see CAPITAL). For a company limited by guarantee, the maximum liability is the amount that the members of the company have guaranteed to pay in the event of LIQUIDATION.

Line management

Those managers who are primarily responsible for the actual production of a COMPANY'S goods and SERVICES. This classification is an analogy to the military, where line duties are those in the front line of fighting, and staff duties are those in support.

In companies, too, staff managers provide support services for the line managers, such as planning, personnel, shipping, and so on. Many find the distinction between line and staff jobs increasingly artificial. There are few line jobs that have no involvement with, say, planning or personnel.

Liquid assets

Any ASSETS that can be quickly turned into cash without loss, for example, bank deposits or government SECURITIES. Many more assets can, of course, be sold quickly, but they are not liquid if the seller would have to incur a loss in order to sell them quickly.

LIQUIDATION

The corporate equivalent of execution and burial, the tidying up of a COMPANY'S affairs when it ceases to do business. This is usually because the company is unable to pay its debts, but it may occur because the owners have decided that the business has achieved what it set out to do.

The corporate undertaker (called the liquidator) is usually an accountant or a lawyer, but not always. His main job is to ascertain the exact amount owed to the company's CREDITORS and then sell the company's ASSETS in order to pay back the creditors as much as possible.

Not all creditors are equal; some have priority over others. Secured creditors are paid first, followed by preferential creditors like the liquidator and the tax collector. The rest follow in order of priority.

LIQUIDITY

The amount of short-term ASSETS held by a business and its ability to turn them into cash at short notice. A COMPANY'S liquidity is said to be high if these assets form a large percentage of its total assets. Liquidity is important to companies in helping them ride out temporary aberrations in their MARKETS or a sudden cash crisis.

Net liquidity is a company's short-term assets minus its short-term LIABILITIES. Various ratios are used to test a company's level of liquidity.

- The ACID TEST: cash and easily realizable assets to current liabilities
- The average time it takes to collect trade debts
- The current ratio: current assets to current liabilities

Bank of America developed a list of nine warning signals that indicate to it that a company is getting into trouble. They are listed from the most to the least common.

- Delays in submitting financial statements
- A decline in bank deposits and an increasing incidence of returned checks
- A failure to perform on other obligations (for example, slow repayment of the personal debt of individual directors)
- An INVENTORY glut
- An increase in delinquent payments with more and more straying past their due date
- Difficulty in arranging meetings or visits
- Legal action against the business
- Increasing number of debtors
- Negative information about the business from its competitors and customers

LOCAL AREA NETWORK

A local area NETWORK (LAN) is a COMPUTER network covering a small geographical area, for example, a government department.

LOCK-OUT

The exclusion, from a FACTORY or office, of one group of employees by another group. Lock-outs usually occur when there are disputes between MANAGEMENT and TRADE UNIONS. Sometimes they are intertwined with a STRIKE. Managers may lock out BLUE-COLLAR WORKERS who decide unilaterally to return to work after a strike.

LOSS LEADER

A product that is sold below COST in order to entice CONSUMERS into buying other products. Loss leaders are a MARKETING device promoted by RETAILERS. A number of manufacturers object to their products being sold as loss leaders.

MACHINE LOADING

The allocation of specific tasks to individual machines within a **FACTORY**, the responsibility of the production **CONTROL** manager.

MACHINE TOOL

A piece of equipment used for cutting or shaping metal. Machine tools range from simple drills and lathes to the sophisticated pieces of equipment required to prepare metal for use in aircraft, cars, or satellites.

MAINTENANCE

The **COST** of keeping **PLANT AND EQUIPMENT** running efficiently. This is generally only the actual cost incurred in servicing the equipment. It does not include the **OPPORTUNITY COST** of having equipment out of operation while it is being serviced.

The worst part about success is trying to find someone who is happy for you.

Old saying

MANAGEMENT

Either the group of managers who together run a business, or the art of so doing. The word "manage" is several centuries old, and it comes from the Italian *manneggiare*, "to handle" (horses). It is widely acknowledged that effective management requires a number of particular abilities.

- To listen as well as to talk
- To lead by example

- To give clear instructions when required
- To select competent people
- To know how to encourage people to be innovative
- To give credit when credit is due
- To be honest, consistent, approachable, and decisive
- To be able to delegate

To manage is to forecast and to plan, to organize, to command, to coordinate and to control.

Henri Fayol

MANAGEMENT BY OBJECTIVES

A popular phrase used to describe MANAGEMENT systems where employees agree jointly with senior managers as to what are to be their objectives (or ultimate goals) in the job. They then track their progress in moving toward those goals with the managers.

MANAGEMENT BY WALKING AROUND

Most famously demonstrated by the COMPUTER COMPANY Hewlett-Packard, management by walking around (MBWA) is a style that emphasizes the importance of face-to-face contact. One great advantage of MBWA is that it removes the expectation among employees that the only time they will see their top managers is when there is trouble and confrontation. (See also MANAGERIAL GRID)

MANAGEMENT DEVELOPMENT

A catch-all phrase referring to the teaching and nurturing of MANAGEMENT skills (for example, team building or negotiation) instead of specific technical skills (like engineering or accounting).

Any systematic training of managers depends on having a clear knowledge of what managers need to do. There are eight functions that are generally agreed to be central to the job of managing.

- Planning
- Organizing
- Staffing
- Supervising
- Directing
- Controlling
- Coordinating
- Innovating

MANAGERIAL GRID

A popular way of classifying MANAGEMENT styles by plotting "concern for results" against "concern for people," each on a scale of 1 to 9. Styles are usually found to polarize around five points on the graph.

1,1: the "impoverished" style. Only concerned with getting necessary work done with minimum effort.

1,9: the "country club" style. People's needs come way ahead of achievement.

9,1: the "scientific management" style. FREDERICK TAYLOR-type concentration on maximizing efficiency.

5,5: the "middle of the road" style. Trying to achieve reasonably good results while keeping employees reasonably happy.

9,9: the "team management" style. Committed workers trying to get the best out of themselves and others.

The grid is useful as a framework for discussion of styles. It cannot be used for a serious quantitative comparison of different companies.

MARGIN

In general, an amount of money "at the edge." In economic theory the margin is that level of production at which the COST of producing one more item is equal to the revenue to be gained from it. Marginal cost is the extra cost of producing one more unit of an article over and above an agreed output.

Margin lending. Lending by banks backed by the VALUE of SHARES. Banks will usually lend up to a certain percentage (about 60%) of the value of shares. If the shares' value declines, the bank will ask the borrower to repay an amount so that the loan remains at 60% of the (lower) value of the shares backing it. This type of lending has gotten many wealthy people into trouble.

Margin trading. The buying of SECURITIES through a BROKER while only putting up part of the cost of the securities, the rest coming as a loan from the broker. In effect this is the eternally dangerous practice of gambling with borrowed money.

Profit margin. The difference between the cost of something and the amount for which it is sold (see MARK-UP). All businesses need to know the full cost of their goods and SERVICES in order to know at what selling price they will have an acceptable profit margin.

MARKET

The place where buyers (that is, demand) and sellers (that is, supply) come together to trade in goods and SERVICES and to determine their prices. Such a place can be as large as a country, "Sales in the U.S. market were weak last year," or as small as a single building, "Traders on the London STOCK MARKET keep bumping into each other." "Market economics" refers to the setting of prices in an economy by markets rather than by regulators or governments.

"Market" can also be the total VALUE of all sales in a market place. Hence "MARKET SHARE" refers to the percentage share of those sales belonging to a product or business—for example, "BMW has an 8% share of the car market in Japan." The market leader is that product or COMPANY with the largest market share.

MARKETING

According to the Institute of Marketing this is "the MANAGE-MENT process of identifying, anticipating, and satisfying customer requirements profitably." Another definition is "the process of taking the guesswork out of hunch."

Marketing includes functions like ADVERTISING, MARKET RE-SEARCH, PRICING, sales promotion, and testing new products ("test MARKETING"). In large companies all these responsibilities often come under a single "marketing" department. In smaller businesses they are either brought in from outside firms (advertising and market research, in particular), or they are the direct responsibility of someone not far from the chief executive.

Not everything that goes by the name of "marketing" deserves it. It has become too fashionable. A grave-digger remains a grave-digger even when called a mortician. Only the cost of burial goes up.

Peter Drucker

MARKET RESEARCH

The process of methodically investigating a potential MARKET for a new product, or of examining the market for an existing product and the way it has changed (or might be about to change). Market research involves asking a sample of people a number of questions about a product, service, or a **COMPANY**. This can be done in many ways: at random on the street, in structured discussion groups, by telephone, or by written questionnaire. The answers are then analyzed statistically in order to examine the (potential) market along a number of different dimensions: age, geography, social status, and so on.

A stable competitive market never has more than three significant competitors, the largest of which has no more than four times the market share of the smallest.

The Boston Consulting Group's "Rule of Three and Four"

MARKET SHARE

A **COMPANY'S** sales in a particular **MARKET** expressed as a percentage of total sales in that market. This is a key indicator of a company's competitive position among its commercial rivals. Japanese companies lay great store by market share, often concentrating on it at the expense of **PROFIT**.

One problem with market share is that it is not always clear what market is being shared. For example, is Hershey competing in the market for chocolate bars, for all chocolate, or even for all candy? It is no good having 80% of the chocolate-bar market if people have stopped buying bars and are eating boxed chocolates instead.

MARK-UP

The profit **MARGIN** related to **COST**. If a **RETAILER** sells something for $125 for which she paid $100, the profit margin is $25, or

20% (one-fifth) of the selling price. The retailer's mark-up is also $25, but it is 25% (one-quarter) of the cost price.

ABRAHAM MASLOW

An influential psychologist who died in 1970. His most famous theory was that of the HIERARCHY of needs in the workplace. In ascending order they were:

- security and self-control
- social relationships
- self-esteem
- status and recognition
- achievement and challenge
- power
- creativity
- self-actualization

The earlier needs on the list have to be satisfied before people can move on to the later ones. Maslow has been criticized for being too idealistic, but his hierarchy does have a common-sense ring of truth about it.

MASS PRODUCTION

The production of large quantities of standard items using ECONOMIES OF SCALE to keep the COST of each item as low as possible. (See also BATCH and JOBBING)

The technology of mass production is inherently violent, ecologically damaging, self-defeating in terms of nonrenewable resources, and stultifying for the human person.

E. F. Schumacher

MASTER'S DEGREE IN BUSINESS ADMINISTRATION

A postgraduate (and usually post-experience) general training in business and MANAGEMENT. In the United States (where most universities now offer degrees in business administration), the Master's Degree in Business Administration (MBA) course usually lasts two years; in Europe it tends to be condensed into one year; and in Japan it does not exist (or it is equivalent to a lifetime of work experience).

Most MBA courses have a core of compulsory subjects plus a number of elective courses from which students can choose those that best suit them. The range of subjects varies, but it usually includes the following staples:

- accounting and finance
- organizational behavior
- marketing
- operations
- human-resource management
- economics and business policy

The electives might include such things as international business, INFORMATION TECHNOLOGY, small businesses, or health services management.

The number of students enrolling for MBA courses has increased rapidly in recent years. The United States now turns out more than 70,000 MBAs every year. At the same time the number of universities and colleges offering MBA courses has increased dramatically. This means that it is more important to a potential employer not if a candidate has an MBA (for they are two a penny), but where it was obtained. An MBA is no longer of itself a passport to a world of six-figure salaries.

MATERIALS HANDLING

A key part of the production process, involving the movement of components and products around a FACTORY, or from one factory to another. The COST of materials handling can account for up to 40% of total manufacturing cost, and it is the cause of many industrial accidents. Efficient materials handling should ensure the following:

- Materials are always moving toward completion.
- Materials must move as short a distance as possible.
- Materials are carried by similar devices.
- Materials are carried with as little effort as possible.

MATRIX STRUCTURE

Most MANAGEMENT STRUCTURE involves managers having two allegiances and order of reporting: to their specialist function and to their general department. For example, the MARKETING manager of the Spanish subsidiary of a German company will be responsible to the marketing department in Germany and also to the chief executive of the Spanish subsidiary. A copywriter on an ADVERTISING campaign will be responsible to the account executive for that campaign and also to the chief copywriter.

This duality is usually expressed in the form of a two-dimensional matrix showing lines of responsibility going both horizontally and vertically.

MEAN

The average of a series of numbers. There are three different types of mean.

1. Arithmetic mean. The sum of all the numbers divided by the number of numbers; the most basic "average."

2. Geometric mean. This is calculated by multiplying all the numbers in the series together and then taking the nth root of that multiple, where n is the number of numbers. The geometric mean is useful where values change over time; it is always less than the arithmetic mean.

3. **Weighted mean.** This is a method of taking account of the fact that not all the numbers in the series will have the same significance. Thus before the mean is calculated, the more important numbers are "weighted." This involves multiplying them by a factor that reflects their importance.

MEETING

The formal gathering together of a number of individuals is a central part of all corporate life. Certain meetings such as board meetings are prescribed by law.

The existence of compulsory meetings at this top level lends them an aura of great significance. "He's in a meeting" is an instant conversation killer. Ask no more; he must be gainfully employed. It is also of course an understandable managerial ploy to fend off the intrusive attack of the telephone. Unfortunately, legislation has never prescribed what should be achieved in a meeting, or how long it should take.

Here are some of the ingredients of a good meeting.

- The right people should be there—their subordinates if appropriate, but no superfluous people.

- Everyone attending the meeting must know in advance the place of the meeting and the agenda.

- There must be a CHAIR present.

- The purpose of the meeting must be stated at the beginning.

- The chair should summarize at various points.

- Each person should have a chance to speak, and no one person should have too much floor time.

- The aims of the meeting must be achieved; stating them is not enough.

- Action points and deadlines must be agreed on at the conclusion of the meeting.

- Minutes of the meeting should be circulated if appropriate.

MENTORING

A method of MANAGEMENT training in which junior managers are assigned a specific individual senior manager to whom they have access for advice and guidance. This is something like the tutorial system practiced in older universities.

MERCANTILISM

A seventeenth-century economic tenet in Europe. National wealth was believed to be accumulated by gaining an excess of exports over imports. Protectionism was justified in order to cut imports, and domestic wages were kept low to increase exports. Pride of place in society went to the trading (mercantile) classes.

Mercantilism gave way in the eighteenth and nineteenth centuries to the laissez-faire, free-market economics of ADAM SMITH and others. The fundamental conflict between the two economic ideas persists in today's shifting calls for protectionism on the one hand and for free trade on the other.

MERCHANT BANK

A financial institution unique to the United Kingdom whose closest equivalent is the U.S. investment bank (see COMMERCIAL BANK). Merchant banks grew up to finance the great traders of the age of MERCANTILISM. Many of them were set up by continental European families, the Rothschilds, Hambros, and Schroders, for example. Today their central role is no longer that of providing trade finance but rather of providing CORPORATE FINANCE and advice.

MERGERS AND ACQUISITIONS

Wall Street and the City of London make much of their money out of mergers and acquisitions (M&A), namely the ways in which companies come together. Mergers are friendly combinations of two companies into a new entity; ACQUISITIONS are (often hostile) takeovers of one COMPANY by another.

The advantage of friendliness in mergers can be counterbalanced by paralysis. Boards of directors may be simply added together; two recently merged Spanish banks created a board of 38 people. Nobody resigns (because nobody "won") and there are no ECONOMIES OF SCALE.

> *I always said that mega-mergers were for megalomaniacs.*
>
> David Ogilvy

MIDDLE MANAGER

An unflattering term referring to the large number of managers who are neither at the top of the managerial ladder nor obviously at the bottom of it. Middle managers are often based at a COMPANY'S head office, filling out the corporate pyramid between the directors and the line managers.

MANAGEMENT gurus have forecast a gloomy future for middle managers. As long ago as 1954 Peter Drucker said that seven layers of management was the most that any company needed. More recently, a report by the top management consultants, McKinsey, said the following:

> *The first step in accomplishing successful plant-floor implementation of new manufacturing approaches is the clearing out of all middle managers and support-service layers that clog the wheels of change.*

MINIMUM WAGE

In some countries governments determine a wage that is the least that any full-time employee can legally be paid. The setting of such a wage encourages the growth of a black MARKET in LABOR, where wages are below the legal minimum and where employees have no legal protection from exploitation.

TRADE UNIONS and MANAGEMENT also sometimes agree between themselves on minimum wages that are to be paid for particular jobs.

MINORITY INTEREST

When a COMPANY owns more than 50% but less than 100% of another company (its SUBSIDIARY), the other shareholders (who own less than 50%) are called "the minority interest." A company's accounts will embrace all its subsidiary company's ASSETS and LIABILITIES. There will be a separate item representing its obligation to the minority shareholders in its subsidiaries.

Minority interests have a degree of legal protection against exploitation by the majority.

MISSION STATEMENT

A statement by a COMPANY of its overriding business goals, of how it is going to achieve them, and of the values it will uphold in doing so.

After a visit to Sears, Roebuck in the 1920s, the founders of Marks & Spencer, then a rather ordinary general store, redefined their mission as follows:

The subversion of the class structure of nineteenth-century England by making available to the working and lower-middle classes, upper-class goods of better than upper-class quality at prices the working and lower-middle classes could well afford.

Few companies have such a precise (or socially ambitious) mission statement.

Much attention has recently been focused on the value of mission statements as a tool for creating team spirit and unity of purpose among a company's workforce by giving workers an idea of a higher purpose to their LABOR. To achieve their aim, mission statements must be:

- the result of some sort of consensus throughout the company of what it is about
- clear and memorable
- widely known and widely disseminated throughout the corporation
- realistic, and not based on some far-flung ambition that employees cannot relate to

MNC

See **MULTINATIONAL COMPANY**

MODEM

A shortened form of modulator-demodulator, the instrument that is attached between a **COMPUTER** and a telephone line to allow computer messages to be converted into telephonic messages and sent long distances. Without the modem there would be no informatics (see **INFORMATION TECHNOLOGY**).

MONOPOLY

The total absence of **COMPETITION**, the situation where a single producer has the whole of a **MARKET** to itself. It is usually assumed that a **COMPANY** that has a monopoly will abuse its position by increasing prices considerably more than they would be if the company had competition. The extra profits from this are called monopoly profits.

How come there's only one Monopolies Commission?

Graffiti

Some monopolies have official approval—for example, those granted by **PATENTS** on new drugs and inventions. These are granted for a limited period, however, and are a reward for the COST of the research that went into originally creating the product.

Monopolies are rarely "pure" in practice for two reasons.

- Very few (if any) products or SERVICES are so self-contained that they are not subject to some competition. The United States's regional newspapers and Europe's nationalized electricity industries are near-monopolies, but the newspapers compete with television and electricity competes with gas.

- Governments make an effort to ensure that those near-monopolies that do exist are not abused. Many nationalized industries have regulatory bodies to CONTROL their prices. TAKEOVERS and ACQUISITIONS in sensitive sectors (such as newspapers) are closely monitored by antitrust authorities.

The great achievement of Mr. Sloan of General Motors was to structure this gigantic firm in such a manner that it became in fact a federation of fairly reasonably sized firms.

E. F. Schumacher

MOTIVATION

What moves people to behave in particular ways. Motivation is an important subject in several business areas. What motivates CONSUMERS to buy one thing and not another? What motivates employees to work hard? What motivates shareholders to be less than indifferent? Here are some useful tips.

- Remember that different people respond to different incentives and styles of MANAGEMENT.

- Manage the overall problem-solving process; let staff manage the problems.

- Work with a team to identify the members' strengths and weaknesses, and encourage them to develop their full potential.
- Involve the team in the early stages of projects.
- Do not keep all the interesting and creative work to yourself.
- Let your team help you.
- Give frequent and specific feedback, both positive and negative.

We were struck by the number of non-monetary incentives used by excellent companies . . . the volume of contrived opportunities for showering pins, buttons, badges, and medals on people is staggering at McDonald's, Tupperware, IBM, and many of the other top performers.

Tom Peters and Robert Waterman, *In Search of Excellence*

MULTINATIONAL COMPANY

A **COMPANY** that has production and **MARKETING** operations in more than one country. Multinational companies (MNCs) are nothing new. In the early years of this century U.S. companies like Kellogg and Singer had several production facilities outside the United States.

However, these early multinationals operated like a series of independent national operations, largely because communications and transport systems were slow and inefficient. Each national business was forced to plan and operate as an independent unit. Only in recent years (with the help of sophisticated air transport and telecommunications) have multinationals come to work more as a single unit across the globe. People have looked for a new word to describe this new type of modern multinational: global company or transnational, for example.

In fact, however, the very global Coca-Cola is still dominated by its headquarters in Atlanta.

MULTINATIONAL ENTERPRISE

Another term for MULTINATIONAL COMPANY, often abbreviated to MNE.

MURPHY'S LAW

The rule in business that if something *can* go wrong, it *will* go wrong.

NATIONALIZATION

The taking over by government of privately owned companies. Nationalization is the opposite of **PRIVATIZATION**, and it is a highly charged political issue. Socialist parties tend to favor nationalization, and conservative parties privatization, though the issue is rarely cut and dried. France's socialist president, François Mitterrand, actually decreased the size of the state's shareholdings in French industry.

There are three occasions when the arguments in favor of nationalization are strong.

1. When a **COMPANY** has a near-**MONOPOLY** in its **MARKET**, and the state takes over in order to prevent the company from taking unfair advantage of its position.

2. When a company is in a sensitive area (such as defense), and it is in a nation's best interests that **CONTROL** of that company does not fall into "undesirable" hands.

3. In new industries, in which a country believes it is strategically important to be involved. but that the **PRIVATE SECTOR** is unable (or unwilling) to nurture. In developed countries this is usually in new **HIGH-TECH** areas like semiconductors; in developing countries it is more often in heavy industries like steel, where the government does not want to be entirely dependent on imports.

If you want to make sure that crime doesn't pay, put it in the hands of the government.

Anon

NEGOTIATION

These are the Harvard Negotiation Project Rules:

- Separate the people you are negotiating with from the prob-lem. Do not let emotions and personalities get in the way, but do let emotions show. This is contrary to the traditional "poker-face" approach to negotiation.

- Focus on interests, not positions. It requires trust to expose your real underlying interest in negotiations, rather than some pose struck to create a particular impression.

- Search for new ideas that will be to both parties' benefit.

- Stick to objective criteria: from financial statements or MAR-KET data.

NET PRESENT VALUE

A mathematical concept used to measure the viability of an investment project. Net present value (NPV) is the difference between the present value of the future revenues of the project and the present value of its future COSTS. The present value is calculated by discounting the future revenues and costs by the cost of CAPITAL.

NETWORK

A system that links a number of COMPUTERS (via a central pro-cessing unit—CPU) so that they can share one DATABASE and gain access to each other's files. Like the word "INTERFACE," network has gained a wider currency from its computer usage. Networking, or making contacts, is what businessmen are sup-posed to be doing when they attend business cocktail parties and overseas conferences.

Networking also means a popular way for service firms (like lawyers and accountants) to build up an international presence without the CAPITAL COST of opening offices in dozens of cities. Linked together under some sort of loose umbrella organization, firms in different countries agree to pool their resources as and when necessary. Loose structures of this sort, however, create problems of their own. Charging for the various little favors that are demanded becomes very difficult. Yet depending on strangers to return favors is unreliable. Inevitably, one partner in the network feels unfairly burdened.

NET WORTH

A COMPANY'S ASSETS less its LIABILITIES. "Tangible net worth" is the same equation, but with INTANGIBLE ASSETS (like GOODWILL) subtracted from the total. Net worth is that part of the company that would be left for its shareholders were all its assets to be sold for the amounts that the accountants claim they are worth. "Net asset backing" is the net worth per SHARE.

NICHE MARKET

A small sector of a MARKET. Apple is in a niche market in the COMPUTER industry, unlike IBM, for example, which aims to be all things to all computer users.

Small innovative businesses are particularly good at identifying niche markets and then settling down cozily in them. Big companies frequently ignore them as being too small to be bothered with, but, as Apple has shown, a carefully identified niche can become a very big market indeed.

NIMBY

See NOT IN MY BACK YARD

NONTARIFF BARRIER

A barrier to trade that is not in the form of a TARIFF imposed on an import at its point of entry. Nontariff barriers can take many forms. At their most crude they come in the form of quotas: ceilings on the quantity of goods or SERVICES that can be imported.

More subtly they take the form of a distribution system that discriminates in favor of locally produced goods—a nontariff barrier that Japan is frequently accused of having—or of government regulation that (in banking, for example) only allows to operate people who are known to the local community.

Another popular nontariff barrier comes in the form of standard safety requirements for products that, by extraordinary coincidence, are only met by locally produced goods. Perhaps the most notorious nontariff barrier in recent commercial history was imposed by the French in 1982 when they insisted that all imports of videotape recorders should pass through Poitiers, a tiny inland customs post that could handle less than a fifth of the amount of videotape recorders that were previously being imported into France from Japan.

NOT IN MY BACK YARD

Jargon to describe the reaction of the individual to a decision by society that something distasteful must be done. Not in my back yard (NIMBY) is particularly prevalent in environmental issues where all governments can agree that waste must be treated in a particular way, and they can also all agree that it must be NIMBY.

NPV

See **NET PRESENT VALUE**

OCR

See **OPTICAL CHARACTER RECOGNITION**

OFFICE AUTOMATION

The introduction of **COMPUTERS**, **FAX** machines, and sophisticated telecommunications equipment into offices. Automation of the office was expected to reduce the need for human **LABOR** in the same way as earlier automation of the **FACTORY** had done, but it seems to have increased the number of office jobs rather than reduced them.

A photocopier is a machine that can reproduce human error flawlessly.

Anon

OFFSHORE

Places that set out to attract foreign-currency financial business by creating a fiscally and legally attractive **ENVIRONMENT** are known as offshore centers. Most of them are on small, warm islands. The definition is somewhat arbitrary, however, since it can embrace the whole of deeply onshore Switzerland.

The best-known offshore centers are members of the Offshore Group of Banking Supervisors, which include Aruba, Bahamas, Bahrain, Barbados, Bermuda, Cayman Islands, Cyprus, Gibraltar, Guernsey, Hong Kong, Isle of Man, Jersey, Lebanon, Malta, Mauritius, Netherlands Antilles, Panama, Singapore, and Vanuatu. They have all endorsed the principle that they should try to prevent the banking system from being used for the purposes of money laundering. Endorsing a principle, however, is very different from preventing a practice.

OLIGOPOLY

The **CONTROL** of an industry by a few producers. Oligopolies can be found in many industries and can behave like a **MONOPOLY**, just as the major oil-producing countries do through **OPEC**. On the other hand they can be fiercely competitive, like Procter & Gamble and Unilever. Between them they dominate the world production of laundry detergents but when one twitches, the other does too.

ON-LINE/OFF-LINE

On-line means having access to a remote location from a **COMPUTER** via a communications link such as a telephone line, and it is in real time. Off-line means that the work is done at a remote location and is only entered on to the central computer periodically, either by downloading from a telephone line or by tape or disk, and therefore this is not in real time.

OPEC

See **ORGANIZATION OF PETROLEUM EXPORTING COUNTRIES**

OPEN PLAN

A form of office design where there are no dividing walls breaking up the space into separate offices. Useful in particular circumstances—in newspaper editorial offices, for example, where it is efficient for everybody to hear what everybody else is doing —open-plan design was a fashion that was taken to extremes. It was often socially divisive. Senior managers remained isolated in individual cubicles, while the rest milled around harboring their grievances. Many open-plan offices were subsequently altered to give individuals more privacy and to cut down on noise.

OPERATIONS MANAGEMENT

The MANAGEMENT of the production systems of a manufacturing business. The expression has extended to the management of the systems of service industries (like banking) since the skills required for both have been found to be similar.

Operations management has traditionally been on the sidelines of corporate decision making. Once decisions have been made on where to site plant and machinery (and how far to automate the process), it has been assumed that there is little more to be done. That view of operations management is similar to flying a jet across the Atlantic: a question of using the autopilot.

Companies have come to realize that operations management can be more closely integrated with other parts of the business, such as MARKETING and new-product development. Then it becomes a competitive weapon rather than a fact of life.

If you don't know where you're going, any road will do.

Old saying

OPPORTUNITY COST

The COST of *not* doing something. Although a key concept in business economics, it is not the sort of cost recognized by accountants. Business always involves making choices, and decision making involves the rejection of opportunities as much as the selection of them. Should a COMPANY'S resources be allocated to launching an existing product into a new MARKET, or a new product into an existing market? Or should the company just put its money in the bank and lay off a few workers? The opportunity cost is the reward that would have come from the best course of action that the business did not follow.

If the choice lies between the production or purchase of two commodities, the value of one is measured by the sacrifices of going without the other.

H. J. Davenport

OPTICAL CHARACTER RECOGNITION

An important breakthrough that could have a significant impact on productivity in a number of businesses. Optical character recognition (OCR) is a technology that enables computers to "read" typescript (and ultimately, perhaps, handwritten script) directly. It thus eliminates the need to rekey material into a COMPUTER.

OPTION

A CONTRACT that gives a person the right to buy or sell a commodity, currency, or security within a given period of time (usually anything up to nine months) at an agreed price, called the striking price. The buyer of the contract pays a small premium for the right to exercise the option.

An option to buy is called a "call option," because the holder of the option has the right to call for the commodity (or whatever) from the taker of the option. An option to sell is called a "put option," because the holder has the right to put the commodity to the taker at the agreed price.

Options give industry and commerce the chance to fix an advance price for the RAW MATERIALS, currency, or financial instruments that they might need. The people who buy their options are usually speculators hoping to make a significant gain from price changes.

There are a growing number of secondary markets where options can be traded between the time that the contract is made and the time that it matures. These give speculators the LIQUIDITY they like to have. This type of option should be distinguished from a stock option, which is the right given by companies to key employees to buy some of the COMPANY'S SHARES at a favorable price. Stock options are given as an INCENTIVE to attract and retain key employees. They cannot be traded.

ORGANIZATIONAL BEHAVIOR

The study of the behavior of individuals, and of groups of individuals, within organizations. This embraces subjects like LEADERSHIP, motivation, and the resolution of conflict.

ORGANIZATION OF PETROLEUM EXPORTING COUNTRIES

Founded in 1960 to represent the interests of the main oil-exporting nations in their dealings with the major oil companies, the Organization of Petroleum Exporting Countries (OPEC) is the only really successful primary-product CARTEL. It controls more than half of the world's traded oil.

ORGANIZED LABOR

Workers who have organized themselves into TRADE UNIONS in order to use the power of COLLECTIVE BARGAINING in NEGOTIATIONS with their employers.

OTC

See OVER THE COUNTER

OUTPLACEMENT

Assistance given by an employer to an employee who is being dismissed. The service is often provided by specialist outplacement agencies whose main task is to find the employee a new job. The agency may also give financial advice, counseling to the dismissed employee's family, and tips on how to handle job interviews or to prepare a resumé.

OUTSOURCING

The obtaining of materials or components from suppliers outside the organization. In rethinking the extent of their VERTICAL INTEGRATION, companies often discover that it is more efficient to buy in components made by others than it is to make those components themselves.

In Japanese manufacturing methods all units in the production process are exhorted to treat the next unit as a customer. This reduces the difference between vertical integration and outsourcing.

OVERHEADS

The COSTS of a business that cannot be directly attributed to the production of particular items. A manufacturer's overheads may include the following:

- administration and personnel departments
- distribution
- finance department
- R&D
- warehousing services

OVER THE COUNTER

An over-the-counter (OTC) MARKET is an informal STOCK MARKET trading SHARES that are not listed on a main stock exchange.

OVERTIME

Work done by employees during hours that exceed the time that has been agreed on with their employer. Overtime is usually paid at a higher rate than normal working hours. Thus, "time and a half" means the normal hourly rate plus 50%; "double time" means twice the normal rate.

PARETO'S PRINCIPLE

Named after Vilfredo Pareto, an Italian professor of political economy in Lausanne in the nineteenth century. His principle (often known as the 80/20 rule) states that a large proportion of the activity in a **MARKET** is always accounted for by a small number of operators. In other words, 80% of a **COMPANY'S** profits come from 20% of its products.

Pareto himself found this to be true of the income distribution of nations, and he discovered (incidentally) that distributions tend to be the same whatever the nation. Extending this brought him to Pareto's Law: the only way to increase the incomes of the poorest members of society is by increasing production, that is the gross domestic product (GDP). In other words, redistribution will not work.

PARKINSON'S LAW

The title of a book, first published in 1958 and written by a history professor called Cyril Northcote Parkinson. The book was one of the first about **MANAGEMENT** to be written in a humorous style, and it made a satirical stab at the self-satisfied behavior of managers within large organizations. It had a very wide influence and was translated into many languages.

The book contained a number of "laws," of which the most famous is probably "Work expands to fill the time available for its completion." Allied to this is the principle that "Expenditure rises to meet income." Others include the observation about management meetings, "The less important the subject, the more animated the discussion."

PARTNERSHIP

Two or more people (the partners) who join together to undertake a business for **PROFIT** without being incorporated as a **COM-**

PANY. Traditionally formed in professions such as accounting and law, partnerships have developed in significantly different ways in different countries. In some countries, for example, a partnership is a recognized legal entity; in others it has no legal existence separate from the existence of the partners themselves.

In general the partners in a partnership will not have the protection of **LIMITED LIABILITY**, except in the case of a so-called limited partnership. There the active (that is, executive) partners have unlimited liability, but they also have a number of "limited" partners. These partners cannot take part in the **MANAGEMENT** of the partnership, but their liability is limited to the amount of **CAPITAL** that they have pledged to provide. Limited partnerships are more popular in continental Europe than they are in the United Kingdom or the United States. In France they are called *société en commandite*, in Germany *Kommanditgesellschaft*.

The partner of my partner is not my partner.

Lawyer's maxim

PATENT

The right granted to inventors to have a **MONOPOLY** on the **MARKETING** of their inventions for a certain specified period of time. The right is registered at a patent office, which first does a search to determine whether the invention is new. While such a search is taking place inventors can sell their products with the postscript "patent pending."

Obtaining patents around the world is such a complicated business that there are professional patent agents to help inventors protect their inventions. Some inventors (like big drug companies) complain that patents (usually given for 15 to 20 years) do not last long enough. By the time the companies have got all the official approvals needed for a drug to be put on sale these days, many years have passed.

To extend the life of their patents, some inventors take out a different patent on each separate aspect of their invention, each is designed to expire on a different date. This is also to frustrate and confuse potential copycats.

Of the 25 companies with the most patents in the world, 11 are Japanese, 10 are American, and only 4 are European.

PAYBACK PERIOD

The time it takes for an asset or investment to pay for itself. For a new machine it will be the time that it takes to save (or earn) as much as the machine cost. The payback will come through more efficient and less costly production, or through greater productivity. For an investment, the payback period is the time it takes for the returns to equal the investment.

PAYROLL TAX

A tax imposed on an organization's paid employees, that is, its payroll. Payroll tax is usually levied as a fixed amount per employee, regardless of salary. Its purpose is to encourage business to use LABOR more efficiently and to become more CAPITAL-INTENSIVE. However, if it merely leaves more people unemployed, it may cost more (in unemployment benefits) than it raises.

PC

See COMPUTER

If hard work were such a wonderful thing, surely the rich would have kept it to themselves?
Lane Kirkland, president, AFL-CIO

P/E RATIO

See PRICE/EARNINGS RATIO

PERFORMANCE

How do you compare the performance of one COMPANY with that of another? The short answer is "you cannot," because there is no one single measure that embraces all the goals that a company has. There are a number of measures, however, that in combination cover most factors.

- Net sales growth
- Operating/trading PROFIT growth
- Operating margins
- INTEREST COVER
- Earnings growth
- RETURN ON CAPITAL
- PRICE/EARNINGS RATIO (for quoted companies)
- ADDED VALUE

PERSONAL IDENTIFICATION NUMBER

The series of digits by which bank teller machines recognize individual customers. The personal identification number (PIN) is a sort of "pass number," in contrast to the "password" favored by the designers of COMPUTER security systems.

PERSONALITY TEST

A method of quickly assessing the character of new recruits. Personality tests have declined in popularity as employers have realized that their usefulness in predicting behavior is limited, although few ever believed that a complete personality could be revealed in five responses to a blot of ink.

Some firms, however, do still use techniques like graphology to help them assess the suitability of candidates for jobs.

PERSONNEL MANAGEMENT

The job of developing employees within a COMPANY so that they make the maximum contribution to its success. This includes a range of tasks such as:

- recruitment and selection of new staff
- TRAINING of new and existing staff
- defining terms and conditions of employment
- wage negotiations

Whereas personnel management used to be concerned mostly with the welfare of employees as individuals, it has recently become more concerned with the MOTIVATION and structure of employees as a group.

A personnel man with his arm around an employee is like a treasurer with his hand in the till.

Robert Townsend

THE PETER PRINCIPLE

The principle that every man or woman eventually rises to his or her level of incompetence. First enunciated by Laurence J. Peter in a book published in 1969, the principle (also known as "cream rises until it sours") has become so embedded in MANAGEMENT discussion that it obviously strikes at something deeply felt.

Managers are presumed to be promoted whenever they do jobs competently. They stop being promoted when their "final promotion" takes them to a job that they do incompetently. Thus Peter's corollary says that "in time, every post tends to be occupied by an employee who is incompetent to carry out its duties." Therefore companies are only kept alive because work is being done by those who have yet to reach their level of incompetence. Peter reveled in the ailments of those who had obtained their final promotion. They included the following:

Filophilia. The frequent opening of new files.

Galloping phonophilia. The use of two or more phones to keep in touch with subordinates.

Papyrophobia. Obsessive clearing of the desk.

He recommended that managers demonstrate "creative incompetence" in order to avoid making that final promotion. One example he gave was of the successful manager who avoided promotion by occasionally parking in the space reserved for the COMPANY'S CHAIR.

PHILLIPS CURVE

A chart first drawn by the New Zealand economist A. W. Phillips in the 1950s. It showed a close relationship between unemployment rates and the change in nominal wage rates in the United Kingdom between 1861 and 1957. For a while this seemed to prove conclusively and sensationally that there was a simple trade-off to be made between INFLATION and unemployment. Sadly, almost as soon as the curve was discovered, it started to go haywire. The close relationship has scarcely ever been discernible since.

PICKET

An employee who, as part of an industrial dispute, stands at the entrance to the employer's place of business and tries to persuade other employees not to go to work. A picket also tries to persuade suppliers not to deliver, and customers not to buy. Within certain limits, peaceful picketing is legal.

When somebody pickets somebody else's place of business it is called "secondary picketing," which is against the law in most countries.

Piece rate

A method of rewarding workers based on the number of units that they produce. It differs from the more common way of paying employees according to the number of hours they work.

On occasions the two methods of rewarding LABOR are combined. Workers receive a MINIMUM WAGE, which is bolstered by a commission on the amount of goods (above a minimum) that they sell or produce. Such a combination is a common way of rewarding salespeople.

Pie chart

A popular way of presenting corporate statistics so that they can be easily understood by the average reader. The whole of a COMPANY'S sales, say, are represented by a whole pie. Slices of the pie can then be cut to represent subgroups of the total sales: either sales broken down by different products or by geographical region.

PIN

See PERSONAL IDENTIFICATION NUMBER

Plant and equipment

A commonly used general expression for everything that is required to carry on an industrial process (tools, machines, robots, and so on) other than the buildings, the people, and the fixtures and fittings (air-conditioning systems and so on).

Point-of-sale

The place where the customer finally gets together with the product (or service) and a sale is made. Originally a point-of-sale was a RETAIL shop, but with the introduction of more sophisticated retailing methods, it has also come to mean a single check-out counter at a supermarket, or an automatic teller machine (an electronic point-of-sale).

PORTFOLIO

A collection of SECURITIES (SHARES or BONDS) from a disparate bunch of companies.

Portfolio investment. The practice of spreading an investor's funds across a wide range of shares to reduce the RISK from any one COMPANY or industry.

Portfolio MANAGEMENT. A way of managing a company as if it were a series of distinct parts, each to be considered as a separate element of a portfolio. Portfolio management has been somewhat pushed aside by the fashion for things "holistic," things considered as a whole.

Also a collection of a person's artistic or graphic work. For example, a designer may ask if you want to see his or her portfolio.

PORTFOLIO THEORY

A study of the way in which individuals and institutions alter their risks by investing in a range (portfolio) of investments and ASSETS. When a pension fund starts buying Impressionist masterpieces or a paper company starts buying SOFTWARE firms, what are they up to? Maximizing returns, or minimizing risks, or something in between?

PORTFOLIO WORK

A way of describing the work of the self-employed specialist who works in a number (a portfolio) of different areas. Some of these may be highly paid, while others give a different sort of reward. For example, someone may work as a COMPUTER consultant, a teacher, and a part-time social worker. Portfolio work is expected to increase as lifetime careers with a single employer become rarer.

POSITIONING

The attempt by marketers to define a distinct set of characteristics that differentiate a product or service from its competitors.

For example, the position of the rental car firm Avis was firmly behind the MARKET leader Hertz. So Avis made a virtue out of being number two with the slogan "We're Number Two. We Try Harder."

PR

See PUBLIC RELATIONS

PREFERENTIAL CREDITOR

A CREDITOR who is owed money by a COMPANY in LIQUIDATION but who has the right to more favorable treatment than other creditors. Such preferential treatment is given to those with a CHARGE on the company's ASSETS; unpaid tax collectors; and wages and salaries, up to a certain limit.

PRESENTATION

If you want to sell your BUSINESS PLAN to the board or a new product to a customer, it is essential to present it well. Verbal presentation must be confident, convincing, and articulate. Documents must be clearly written, contain all the necessary information, and look professional. A good idea can be lost if it is badly presented.

PRICE/EARNINGS RATIO

The ratio of a COMPANY'S STOCK MARKET price (P) to its earnings (E). The P/E ratio is a very closely watched figure among stockbrokers and investment bankers. It is supposed to give some indication of whether a company's SHARES are undervalued or overvalued.

The P/E ratio compares a company's stock market value (that is, its number of shares multiplied by its share price) with its latest annual after-tax PROFITS. Put that the other way around, and the ratio is a measure of how many years it would take an investor to get her money back if the company kept profits constant and distributed them all every year. Some hot stocks of the 1980s had P/E ratios of over 30 on the assumption that their profits were going to double or triple over the next few years; in other words, they were not going to stay constant.

PRICING

The difficult task of determining the price of a product. A careful calculation of COSTS can put a floor to that price, but what should be the profit margin added on top? To some extent it will be determined by COMPETITION, but it will also be determined by the costs of distribution, by the POSITIONING of the product, and by the ECONOMIES OF SCALE that can be reaped by selling larger volumes.

PRINTOUT

The printed-on-paper version of electronic COMPUTER data. Early machines for producing printouts were called "daisy-wheel printers." They had a wheel with sprockets that channeled suitably perforated paper in front of the printing head and ribbon. New computer-printing technology (using little jets of ink rather than carbon ribbons) may make the daisy wheel obsolete.

PRISONER'S DILEMMA

A way of showing how an individual's interests and those of the group to which they belong are not necessarily common. Imagine a group of prisoners charged with the same offense and held separately, one to a cell. There are three things that each of them can do.

- He can turn state's evidence while the others keep quiet. He will then become the key witness for the prosecution and be freed while the others are heavily punished.
- He can keep quiet and, provided all the others do the same, all will get a light sentence for lack of evidence.
- He can confess, along with all the others, and they will all get a stiff sentence.

Individually, each prisoner has an incentive to confess in the hope of getting off altogether. But if everybody confesses then they will collectively get a heavier sentence than if they had all kept quiet.

PRIVATE SECTOR

The private sector is that part of business owned by private individuals, that is, not owned or run by government. PRIVATIZATION switches a COMPANY from the PUBLIC SECTOR to the private sector.

PRIVATIZATION

The process of selling off the SHARES in a state-owned business to the PRIVATE SECTOR. Following the gospel of Margaret Thatcher in the early 1980s, many countries were converted to privatization. However, all too rapidly they came up against the privatizer's dilemma: the fact that the businesses the state most wants to sell are those that the private sector least wants to buy, unless sold as a near MONOPOLY.

Privatization is seen as a way of injecting COMPETITION and entrepreneurship into fossilized state-owned monopolies. Whatever it is, it is certainly not an overnight cure. A utility employing hundreds of thousands of people does not become dashing and dynamic overnight because some pieces of paper change hands. The MANAGEMENT'S frame of mind has to change, too.

PRODUCT DEVELOPMENT

Something all companies need to do if they are to be successful. All products have a useful or finite life, so new products must be developed to replace dying ones.

The Economist's marketing department lists ten points to consider when embarking on a new project or product.

- Current situation: where are you now?
- Objectives: Where do you want to be?
- Competition: Who else wants to be there?

- Feasibility: Can you realistically get there?
- Method: How will you get there?
- Resources: What do you need to help you get there?
- Time scale: How long will it take to get there?
- Fall-back positions: What happens if you get delayed or side-tracked?
- Threats and opportunities: What might stop you or help you?
- Longer-term plans: What do you do after you've gotten there?

Finally, draw all these together in a plan or a map to work from.

PRODUCTION LINE

See ASSEMBLY LINE

PRODUCTIVITY

One of those common business words that has been taken over by economists and given a very precise meaning: the output produced in a stated period of time by each unit of any of the three factors of production (land, LABOR, and CAPITAL). Here are some examples:

- the number of tons of wheat produced per year by an acre of land (land productivity)
- the number of widgets manufacturered by one worker in a widget factory in a year (the productivity of labor, and the easiest to measure)
- (less commonly) the money earned on each dollar invested for a year (the productivity of capital)

PRODUCT LIABILITY

The principle that a manufacturer has to pay for damage that occurs as a result of somebody using its products. In the United States product liability awards in the courts can be enormous. In the EUROPEAN COMMUNITY a DIRECTIVE on product liability should soon raise awards and harmonize practice throughout the EC.

PROFIT

To accountants, it is the excess of a COMPANY's revenues over its COSTS. If a company's costs exceed its revenues for a period, then it has made a loss.

To economists, profit is the reward to ENTREPRENEURS for taking the RISKS of doing business: what is left from the price of goods when rewards have been paid to the factors of production, such as salaries to LABOR, rent for land, and interest on CAPITAL.

The accountants' profit is far from being very precise. Whenever two accountants look at one company's books they find three profits. The uncertainty increases because of the many different ways of using the word profit.

After-tax profit. The gross profit less tax.

Gross profit. The profit before the deduction of things like tax and extraordinary items.

MONOPOLY profit. The exceptional profit that a firm can earn if it has a monopoly in a MARKET.

Net profit. The gross profit less tax and other exceptional payments.

Paper profit. A profit that has been earned but not yet realized, like that from the rise in the SHARE price of a company whose shares an investor has not yet sold.

Retained profit. The profit that is left to the company after absolutely everything else has been paid.

---

*What profiteth it a man if he gain the whole world,
yet lose his own soul?*

The Bible

Windfall profit. An unexpected profit that suddenly appears from nowhere (through a DEVALUATION, perhaps, or the death of Uncle Tom).

It is not the aim of Marks & Spencer to make more money than is prudent.

Lord Rayner, when chairman

PROFITABILITY

The ability of a COMPANY to make PROFITS, often loosely used as a synonym for profits themselves: "The company's profitability was high last year," to wit, "it made a lot of profit."

There is an important distinction between PROFIT and profitability: a company that sets out to maximize its profit is not going to maximize its profitability. Maximum profits are obtained when a company is producing at the MARGIN, when the COST of the last unit of output was just less than its revenue. Maximum profitability occurs long before that, when the difference between cost and revenue is a maximum.

PROFIT CENTER

A self-contained part of an organization that is accountable for its own PROFITS and losses. This is not as straightforward as it sounds. In order to be accountable it has to work out the COSTS and revenues associated with the goods and SERVICES that it buys and sells from other parts of the organization, such as payroll services.

PROFIT MARGIN

See MARGIN

PROFIT SHARING

An arrangement between the employees and the owners of a business whereby the employees receive an agreed amount of the COMPANY'S PROFIT. Such schemes sound splendid in theory, a direct financial INCENTIVE for MANAGEMENT to maximize the reward to EQUITY.

In practice, profit-sharing schemes fall victim of all sorts of little jealousies. One of the most common is between those departments that know they made the biggest contribution to profits and those that do not believe the figures.

The idea of making workers share in profits is a very attractive one and it would seem that it is from there that harmony between capital and labor should come. But the practical formula for such sharing has not yet been found.

Henri Fayol

PROGRAM

The series of steps taken by a COMPUTER to solve a particular problem. The person who feeds a computer with the raw data on which the program is to work is called a computer programmer.

PROTECTIONISM

Any obstacle to trade that attempts to put a domestic producer at an advantage over its foreign competitors (see TARIFF). The experience of many countries has shown that protectionism may be helpful to local industry in the short term, but in the long term it cuts them off from progress and change. It can leave local firms extremely vulnerable when the protectionism is removed.

*American-made parts now constitute a smaller
portion of the top models of General Motors, Ford,
and Chrysler than they do of Honda's top models.*

Provision

What nuts are to squirrels, provisions are to accountants:
money put aside out of the harvest of current PROFITS to be
consumed in the future.

Provisions come in two shapes, general and specific. Specific
provisions are set aside against future LIABILITIES that can be
determined with a reasonable degree of accuracy and with a
reasonable degree of certainty that they will happen. General
provisions are set aside against nothing more definite than past
experience of the general level of the industry's liabilities.

Public company

A COMPANY that is allowed to market its SECURITIES, usually
through a stock exchange. The precise nature of public and private companies differs from country to country. In the United
States a public company is one that is registered with the SECU-
RITIES AND EXCHANGE COMMISSION. In Europe there are a number of near-equivalent names and abbreviations.

France	*Société à responsabi-* *lité limitée* (SARL)	*Société anonyme* (SA)
Germany	*Gesellschaft mit* *beschrankter Haf-* *tung* (GMBH)	*Aktiengesellschaft* (AG)
Italy	*Società a responsabi-* *lità limitata* (SRL)	*Società per azioni* (SPA)
Netherlands	*Besloten vennoot-* *schap* (BV)	*Naamloze vennoot-* *schap* (NV)

| Spain | *Sociedad de responsibilidad limitada* (SRL) | *Sociedad anónima* (SA) |
| United Kingdom | Private company | Public limited company (PLC) |

PUBLIC PROCUREMENT

The way in which national governments and PUBLIC-SECTOR bodies place orders for large-scale CONTRACTS like building dams, making soldiers' boots, or building an electricity grid. There are several peculiar features about these contracts.

- Because of their size, firms often get together as a CONSORTIUM in order to be big enough to bid for them.

- So big are the numbers that firms can easily end up working for just one customer (a single government department). That is a monopsony (where there is a single buyer), as opposed to a MONOPOLY (where there is a single supplier), and it leaves the firm exposed to high risks.

- Governments looking at tenders for public procurement contracts have traditionally favored their own national firms. The EUROPEAN COMMUNITY is trying to open up public procurement so that firms from anywhere within the Community get equal treatment with national firms.

PUBLIC RELATIONS

The art of presenting an organization's views and interests in as favorable a light as possible to its many different constituencies: investors, customers, employees, legislators, environmentalists, and so on. Some companies employ outside public relations (PR) consultants; others employ full-time specialists in-house. The very largest companies often use a combination of both.

The traditional way to reach external audiences is through the media—the press, television, and radio—via press releases, press conferences, and INTERVIEWS with key people in the organization. Journalists and public-relations managers have a love/hate relationship: the information that the PR manager wants to give is rarely the information that the journalist wants to receive.

Public relations within organizations, via in-house magazines, is a rapidly growing aspect of the business. So too is INVESTOR RELATIONS, which is concerned with the relationship between a public COMPANY and its large (and constantly changing) group of shareholders.

PUBLIC SECTOR

That part of a nation's economy that is owned and run by government (the opposite of PRIVATE SECTOR). In a communist country virtually the whole of the economy was in the public sector. When there is a substantial private sector as well, an economy is said to be "mixed." There is no economy with no public sector.

PURCHASING POWER

The capacity of CONSUMERs to spend money on goods and SERVICES. Hence the amount of goods and services that consumers can buy with a given unit of currency.

Purchasing power parity (PPP) is the EXCHANGE RATE between two currencies calculated according to how many units of each currency are required to buy an identical basket of goods and services in each currency's country.

QUALITY CIRCLE

A system devised by the Japanese whereby workers are grouped into teams. Each team is responsible for undertaking certain tasks and for the quality of those tasks. The leader of a team is called the "circle facilitator." In the early 1980s quality circles (QCs) were seen as the panacea for all the labor-relations ailments of the Western world.

To their surprise, many Western companies encountered fierce resistance to QCs among their employees. This was largely because they were imposed willy-nilly onto existing organizational structures and were seen to be creating great disruption for little benefit.

QCs then gave way in popularity to **TOTAL QUALITY MANAGEMENT**, a U.S.-inspired method (hijacked by the Japanese) that attempts to integrate quality into existing **MANAGEMENT** structures.

Quality is not an absolute value. It is always based upon and measured according to the expectations of the user.

Gebrüder Sulzer AG, mission statement, The European Foundation for Quality Management

---

QUALITY CONTROL

The testing of a sample of products before they are shipped to a buyer in order to see if they are of the specified quality. A certain tolerance of error may be acceptable in the sample (say, 5%). Above that, buyers will demand further checks. If the faults are large and extensive, they can refuse to take the goods.

It is difficult for companies that are importing goods from far away to carry out rigorous quality-control checks, but there are firms that specialize in doing this on behalf of buyers. By far the biggest in this business is a Swiss firm called SGS, Société Générale de Surveillance.

Nowadays more and more companies realize that it is pointless to learn at the end of the production process—just before they are due to take delivery—that their goods are of poor quality. It is much better for quality control to begin at the moment when the very first step in the production process is taken.

Quality is remembered long after the price is forgotten.

Gucci slogan

QUESTION MARK

One of the four categories in the famous BOSTON MATRIX. A question mark is a COMPANY in a high-growth sector but with low MARKET SHARE. The question: Is it worth persisting with? And if so, what should be done to increase its market share?

QUORUM

The minimum number of people required to hold an official meeting (such as a COMPANY BOARD meeting). If a quorum is not present, any decisions made at the meeting are invalid.

QUOTED COMPANY

A COMPANY whose SHARES are traded on a stock exchange. A company joins the list of other companies "listed" on the stock exchange when dealers on the floor of the exchange "quote" a price for its shares, a price at which they are prepared to trade in those shares.

R&D

See **RESEARCH AND DEVELOPMENT**

RATE OF RETURN

The reward from an investment expressed as a percentage of the original investment, including both **CAPITAL** gain and income. This provides a crude way of comparing the relative attractions of a number of investments. Is it more rewarding to place $10,000 today in an interest-earning bank account and leave it there for five years or to give it to your nephew for his new Guatemalan fast-food business which he hopes to sell to a **PUBLIC COMPANY** in five years' time?

The rate of return is a crude method of comparison because it takes no account of time. Most of the reward from the fast-food business will come as capital gain in five years' time. The reward from the bank is the interest paid at regular intervals throughout the five years.

One method of trying to take account of time in such calculations is called **DISCOUNTED CASH FLOW**. It reduces all the elements of the reward to their **NET PRESENT VALUE**, what they would be worth if they were to be received in cash today. Then in any calculation of rates of return, apples are properly being added to apples.

Note also that the rate of return takes no account of differing degrees of certainty. The bank interest is relatively safe; the nephew's prospective capital gain is not.

RATIO

The relationship between two quantities, expressed either as a percentage or as the multiple of one to the other. Ratios are a favorite tool of financial analysts for comparing one accounting item with another, for example, the ratio of net **PROFIT** to sales.

Such ratios are useful for comparing financial aspects of one COMPANY with another, but they have their limitations. There is no absolutely right ratio for any two things in a company's accounts. So a deviation from the industry average may be significant, but it may equally well not be.

Some favorite ratios are as follows:

Acid test. (Also known as the "quick ratio.") The ratio of a company's cash and quickly realizable ASSETS to its current LIABILITIES.

DIVIDEND cover. The ratio of a company's dividend payment to its net profit.

PRICE/EARNINGS RATIO. The ratio of a company's SHARE price to its earnings per share (EPS).

RATE OF RETURN.

RAT RACE

A colloquial expression for the perpetual struggle of individuals to be successful in their working lives. What people look forward to leaving behind when they retire. The names comes from the curious notion that anything to do with the long-tailed rodent is unpleasant. For example, people who carry on working during a STRIKE are referred to as "rats" when they are not being referred to as "scabs."

RAW MATERIALS

The most primitive inputs into an industrial process. In many cases these are minerals or agricultural materials that have come straight from the ground.

Sometimes they are semiprocessed materials. Silicon chips are the raw material of the COMPUTER industry, for example.

RECEIVER

Somebody appointed by a court to "receive" a troubled COMPANY'S ASSETS on behalf of its DEBENTURE holders (usually its bankers). Receivers, normally accountants or lawyers, are presented with an all-or-nothing choice. Either they try to get the bank's money back by running the company for a while in the hope of turning it round. Or, the more popular and quicker option, they liquidate the company immediately.

Legal procedures like CHAPTER 11 aim to adjust the balance in such situations in favor of creditors other than debenture holders.

RECONCILE

To make a COMPANY'S various sets of books agree with each other and be mutually consistent. To do so, you may also have to reconcile yourself to a touch of fantasy.

RECRUITMENT

The business of identifying and selecting new employees, often from a particular group of the population, as in "graduate recruitment."

RECYCLING

The art of reusing materials that would otherwise be thrown away. Although most publicity on recycling is focused on attempts to reuse household waste such as paper, glass, or aluminum, the majority of recycling is done in industry. Worthwhile savings can be made from retrieving expensive chemicals and from recycling paper in large offices.

Here are tips for setting up a recycling program in an office (taken from *The Green Consumer Guide*, John Elkington and Julia Hailes, London, 1988).

- Appoint an enthusiastic coordinator.

- Find a local wastepaper merchant who will collect the waste.

- Find suitable storage space; 2 square meters per 1,000 square meters of office space is suggested.

- Set up a system of color-coded bins for different types of paper.
- Constantly monitor the system's performance and look for ways to improve it.

RELOCATION

Moving elsewhere. Most managers who join a large organization do not expect to live in one area for the whole of their careers. They may be relocated as individuals to another part of their firm in another part of the country (or, indeed, in another country). Or the part of the firm that they work for may itself be relocated to another part of the country (where LABOR is cheaper or where the firm is closer to important new MARKETS). In very large firms, relocating employees around the world can call for the highest logistical skills.

REPLACEMENT COST

The COST of replacing as asset today. Replacement-cost accounting attempts to draw up a COMPANY'S accounts using replacement cost as the basis for valuing all the company's ASSETS. So all machinery and buildings are valued at the price it would cost to buy them today, not the price at which they were bought originally.

The alternative, HISTORIC-COST accounting, is more objective and simpler but (perhaps) theoretically less pure.

RESEARCH AND DEVELOPMENT

The crucial part of any modern industry, in which scientists and designers search for new products and for new ways of developing existing products. Research refers to the work of pure scientists, chemists, and engineers, for example. Development is more concerned with creating marketable products out of the findings of the researchers.

Expenditure on research and development (R&D) does not bring immediate returns. Scientists and their laboratories are working for future **PROFITS**. In most fields it takes 10 to 20 years from the dawning of an idea to its full commercial **MARKETING**. That is at least twice as long as the average life span of a chief executive.

Some industries are more dependent on R&D than others. The pharmaceutical industry's success is closely related to the ability of white-coated scientists to come up with new drugs in their laboratories. It can cost $50 million and more in R&D to produce an effective new drug, but success is well rewarded. The discovery of the anti-ulcer drug Zantac completely transformed the fortunes of Glaxo.

Japanese companies are famous for their development rather than their research. It is sometimes assumed that this is a rather inferior skill, but a reassessment of the **VALUE** of development is long overdue. Great breakthroughs in research are rare; the **COMPANY** that continually develops its existing products is more assured of a long and successful future.

At 3M every scientist devotes 15% of his or her time to projects of his or her own choice.

RESERVES

Amounts of money that are set aside out of **PROFITS**. The distinction between reserves and provisions is not always clear. Reserves are set aside voluntarily out of profits (and belong to the **COMPANY'S** shareholders); provisions are set aside as a prudent bit of accounting to cover an expected future liability (or future decrease in the **VALUE** of an asset, which is the same thing). The value of the shareholders' stake in a **COMPANY** is its **CAPITAL** plus its reserves.

RESTRAINT OF TRADE

That part of a CONTRACT that imposes a restriction on one of the parties to the contract. Such restrictions usually take one of two forms.

- A restriction on a buyer's ability to purchase goods elsewhere. For instance, for decades many of the United Kingdom's famous pubs were "tied" to buying beer from only one manufacturer. A "free house" was a pub that was free to buy its beer from several suppliers. It usually advertised the fact on its sign outside.

- A restriction on an employee's capacity to work subsequently for a competitor.

In many countries contracts that contain a restraint of trade are legally invalid, unless the contract is between parties of roughly equal bargaining power who are in a position to look after themselves. It is also acceptable if there is good reason for the restraint, for example, if an employer is merely protecting the legal right to its trade secrets or PATENTS.

RESTRICTIVE PRACTICES

Any business practice that restricts free COMPETITION. In free-market economies governments keep a close eye on such practices. Restrictive practices come in many forms. They can be agreements between manufacturers (and distributors) to sell products or SERVICES at a fixed price (known as resale price maintenance). Such agreements exist in Europe, for example, in book retailing. Restrictive practices are also common (though less so than they once were) among the so-called professions.

MANAGEMENT and TRADE UNIONS sometimes collude in restrictive practices by deciding that, for example, two people are required to do a particular job regardless of the fact that advances in technology mean that it can be done perfectly well by one person.

It is often difficult to tell the difference between perfect competition and a restrictive practice. For example, do banks charge exactly the same for their various services because they collude in fixing their prices? Or do they charge the same because competition between them is so perfect that no one of them can afford to be out of line with the others?

RETAILER

The person who stands at the end of the industrial process selling goods to the final consumer in shops, supermarkets, department stores, or stalls. A retailer may also be a WHOLESALER and in some cases even a manufacturer. It is rare for big stores to have their own factories, but many have goods made specially for them (i.e., by original equipment manufacturers). In food retailing the "own-label" brands of the big supermarket chains are presenting a serious threat to traditional manufacturers of things like canned vegetables.

RETURN ON CAPITAL

The RATE OF RETURN on CAPITAL; in particular, the relationship between the net PROFIT of a business and the paid-up SHARE capital of the business. This is a measure whereby shareholders can find out if their money would have been better deposited in a bank, but it is a measure to be wary of. There are almost as many ways of calculating profit as there are of calculating capital.

RETURN ON SALES

The relationship between sales and PROFIT. (See MARGIN)

REWARD SYSTEM

The relationship of rewards within an organization. For example, there is a traditional conflict between the rewards of highly trained specialists and those of general managers. On rare occasions a specialist will earn more than the chief executive. This occurs in the finance industry, for instance, where dealers' rewards are often tied to performance, and their bosses' are not.

A central relationship in reward systems is that between the pay of the highest-paid executive and the average pay of the workforce. In Japan this ratio rarely exceeds 10:1, while in some firms in the United States the chief executive can receive 100 times as much money as the average employee of that firm—and sometimes even more.

Rights issue

An offer of new SHARES for cash to existing shareholders in proportion to the size of their stake in the COMPANY. For example, a one-for-three rights issue entitles every holder of three shares to buy one more at a special price.

Rights issues are popular in good times as a "cheap" way to fund new investment or to pay for MERGERS AND ACQUISITIONS. They are also popular in bad times to replace expensive debt or to take advantage of bargain ACQUISITIONS.

Their main disadvantages are:

- It is a long time before the issuing company gets the cash.
- Since they are usually offered at a DISCOUNT, rights issues raise less cash than the face VALUE of the shares.
- They are administratively tricky if the issuing company has a particularly large number of shareholders.

Risk

The amount that stands to be lost by a certain action or investment. This may be measured in monetary terms: "He risked thousands on that research," or in nonmonetary terms: "He risked his reputation by employing Joe." The main calculation in all business is the set-off between risk and reward. Is the degree of risk involved in doing something justified by the potential reward?

RISK ANALYSIS

Business life is full of all sorts of risk, and analyzing whether it is worth taking a particular risk is the bread and butter of many managers' lives.

Banks spend much of their time analyzing the financial riskiness of companies, and they have five key factors that they watch out for.

- The variability of a COMPANY's CASH FLOW
- The growth of its cash flow
- The company's "interest coverage"; that is, its cash flow divided by the amount it pays in interest
- Its debt maturity, as measured by the percentage of total debt due within one year
- Its LIQUIDITY: the company's current ASSETS divided by its current LIABILITIES

ROBOTICS

The development of machines (called robots) to do work formerly done by humans. The automobile industry in particular uses robots extensively throughout the manufacturing process. Fiat is probably the world's biggest manufacturer of robots.

ROYALTIES

Money paid to somebody else for the use of certain types of property, for example, paying the owner of land for the right to extract minerals from the land; an author for the right to publish his book; or the owner of a patent for use of the item patented.

SALARY SCALE

A table that shows the salaries paid to employees at different levels (grades) in an organization. The scale may define salaries within a particular grade according to rank, length of service, special skills (such as languages), and time spent in the grade.

Few organizations are sufficiently rigid to find salary scales as useful as they are to civil servants, but companies have to make some sort of evaluation of different jobs within their organization, and salary scales are simply a quantification of that process.

Salaries for some jobs can be largely determined by the general **LABOR MARKET**, but these are the commodity-type jobs in computing and **BOOKKEEPING**, for example. For the jobs whose **VALUE** lies largely in experience and knowledge of a particular firm, salary scales are almost unavoidable.

One problem with salary scales is accepting who sets the scales for the people who set the scales? Is it just coincidence that the salaries of executive directors and chief executives (who usually set the scales) so often seem to fly right off the top of the scales that they set?

That's the American way. If little kids don't aspire to make money like I did, what the hell good is this country?

Lee Iacocca, when asked how he reconciled his $20.6 million compensation in 1986 with Chrysler's cuts in pay for other employees.

SALE AND LEASEBACK

An agreement between a business and a property investor whereby the business sells land or buildings that it owns to the investor and then immediately leases them back (see LEASING). The business receives a large CAPITAL sum and, in return, starts paying regular rent to the investor.

Such agreements release the capital tied up in business premises, freeing it for more productive purposes. Sale and leaseback deals are attractive to speculators who buy companies solely for their idle property. The property is sold and leased back, and the cash can then be used to buy another bigger company in a similar position, and so on ad infinitum.

SBU

See STRATEGIC BUSINESS UNIT

FRITZ SCHUMACHER

An unconventional German-born economist who spent much of his life working for the United Kingdom's National Coal Board. He published an influential collection of essays in 1973 that ensured that his reputation would live long after him and that introduced a new phrase to the English language. The collection was entitled *Small Is Beautiful*.

The essays were heavily influenced by the time that Schumacher spent advising the Burmese government in the late 1960s. Among other things he advocated the use of INTERMEDI-ATE TECHNOLOGY by third world countries instead of a sudden leap into heavy industry. At the time, developing countries believed that they had no option but to follow the belching-chimney, ASSEMBLY-LINE model of INDUSTRIALIZATION that had been followed in Europe and the United States.

Like many influential management writers, Schumacher came out with ideas that suited their time. In the early 1970s the corporatist state, a mass of huge private and state-owned companies, seemed to have come to a grinding halt. It needed to be reminded that small could be beautiful.

SEC

See SECURITIES AND EXCHANGE COMMISSION

SECURITIES

Originally the documents that gave evidence of the ownership of investments like SHARES or BONDS. Now it has come to mean the investments themselves: "The art MARKET last year was dead, but securities had a whale of a time."

Since security is also the backing given by a borrower to a lender for a loan (property in the case of a mortgage), some prefer the word "security" not to be used to refer to shares. Ironically, shareholders are the one type of investor with absolutely no security to back the securities they have bought, or "the only security they have is their security."

SECURITIES AND EXCHANGE COMMISSION

The powerful policeman of securities MARKETS. Based in Washington, D.C., the Securities and Exchange Commission (SEC) relies heavily on disclosure of information to do its job. Public companies have to disclose far more to the SEC than they do anywhere else in the world. Many companies shy away from being a QUOTED COMPANY for this reason.

SEED MONEY

The very first small investment in a project. Though unlikely to be enough to get the project fully off the ground, it is sufficient to finance, say, a bit of MARKET RESEARCH that will convince a bank to back the project.

Everyone lives by selling something.

Robert Louis Stevenson

SEGMENTATION

The categorizing of CONSUMERS into a number of different segments, each of which has a distinctive feature. The classification may be according to basic demographic features, such as age, sex, country of residence, and so on. Or it may be done according to less precise "lifestyle" criteria, such as Yuppies, "baby-boomers," or "empty-nesters."

The purpose of segmentation is to identify more precisely the target MARKET for a particular product or service. Surprisingly few products can genuinely hope to appeal to everybody. Even something like beer is consumed largely by a relatively small number of young males with a very distinctive lifestyle.

SEMICONDUCTOR

A substance (like silicon) that "conducts" an electric current less efficiently than metal but more efficiently than an insulator (like rubber), that is, a semi-efficient conductor. Such materials are the bedrock of COMPUTER science.

SENSITIVITY ANALYSIS

The study of how sensitive a set of assumptions is to variations. Applied to a BUSINESS PLAN, for example, sensitivity analysis would consist of asking some "what if" questions. In the plan will be a number of assumptions about such things as future sales, wages, transport costs, and so on. What happens if sales are, say, 10% less than was assumed for the year after next? What if wages increase by 15% instead of the assumed 10% for that year?

From the answers to these questions can be built a matrix of possible outcomes for the business. This will show how sensitive the plan is to different variables and what is the "worst-case scenario." This might be so horrendous that the plan is abandoned altogether, even though it looks potentially profitable should things go reasonably well.

SERVICES

There used to be a clear distinction between goods (which you could touch and weigh) and services (which you could not). Companies did either one or the other, and the importance of services in developed economies was growing dramatically. In West Germany services represented 40% of total output in 1950, and 50% in 1980.

The distinction between goods and services, however, is now blurred. Not only are hairdressers (a service) making their own shampoos (goods), but people are realizing that there were always big chunks of traditional manufacturing businesses that were services: the personnel, accounts, or shipping departments, for example. The service element of manufacturing is increasing as COMPUTERS spread knowledge (and with it the ability to provide service) to everybody, while robots free them from manual drudgery.

Airline passenger to steward: "You're one of the stupidest people I've ever met." Steward: "And you're one of the nicest gentlemen I've ever met. But perhaps we're both wrong."

Swissair training: ideal response to neurotic passenger

SETTING-UP COST

The COST involved in changing a set of machines from producing one product to producing something else. Most of this cost lies in the amount of time that the machines and the people operating them are idle while the change is taking place.

SEVEN SS

Seven qualities (each beginning with the letter S) that were identified in a best-selling book (*The Art of Japanese Management*) as being the areas in which Japanese companies excelled over U.S. companies. The book was written by Richard Pascale in 1981, a year before the even better-selling *In Search of Excellence* by Peters and Waterman. All three had worked together at McKinsey MANAGEMENT consultants, where they had gleaned much of the basic research for their respective books.

The Seven Ss were STRATEGY, structure, systems, shared values, skills, and staff. The first three were called the hard Ss; the last four, the soft Ss. The Japanese made the hard Ss more productive by allying them better with the soft Ss than did Western companies.

SHARE

The CAPITAL of most companies is divided into many small parts called shares. "The capital of ABC, Inc., is divided into 3,000 shares of $4 each." The reward to people who buy shares (shareholders) is an annual DIVIDEND.

SHIFT

A group of employees who work together for a fixed period of time. Shifts are used in industrial processes where work is required during and beyond the normal working day. This may be because it is expensive to shut down machinery every night, and the product of operating for 24 hours a day can all be sold. Or it may be because the nature of the work (some sorts of retailing, for example) demands that it stretch beyond the standard day. There are three main patterns of shift work.

The double-day shift. Two eight-hour periods stretching from 6:00 a.m. to 10:00 p.m.

Three eight-hour shifts. Usually called the morning shift, the afternoon shift, and the night (or "graveyard") shift.

The part-time shift. One that takes over in the evenings for a number of hours after the normal day shift has finished work.

Shifts are sometimes rotated, with one shift working an eight-hour day for two weeks before doing the antisocial eight-hour shift through the night for one week. In general, however, shift workers prefer not to be rotated, but then it becomes difficult and expensive to hold a permanent night shift together.

Shifts are often introduced for short periods when demand is exceptionally high—just before the Christmas holidays, for instance.

SHOP FLOOR

Literally, the FACTORY floor on which a COMPANY'S main production takes place; but also the body of workers who make that production possible, as in "he rose from the shop floor to become managing director."

SHRINKAGE

The reduction in stocks or output because of:

* shoplifting
* the disappearance of goods during transit
* careless handling
* bad workmanship

A certain percentage of production inevitably disappears in shrinkage, but a careful eye needs to be kept on that percentage. Any sudden change may be because a thief has joined the COMPANY or because QUALITY CONTROL has slipped.

SINGLE MARKET

A program devised by the European Commission and intended to turn the 12 members of the EUROPEAN COMMUNITY into a true "single market" by the end of 1992. The idea of Europe as a "common market" was always fundamental to the EC, but progress toward that goal was very slow in the 1970s and early 1980s.

The single-market program gave progress a boost and was helped greatly by two contemporaneous agreements among the EC member states.

- They agreed to accept majority voting among themselves on many issues instead of the previously required unanimous vote.

- They agreed to accept the principle of mutual recognition. That meant nations could say to each other, "I will accept your qualifications (to be an architect or whatever) if you will accept mine." Previously they had attempted to draw up a set of uniform rules that everybody would accept. Needless to say, that usually proved to be impossible.

The single-market program consisted of almost 300 directives removing various barriers to the free movement of CAPITAL, LABOR, and goods between the 12 member states.

By 1992 a large number of these directives had still to be passed by the European Council of Ministers. There was an even larger number waiting to be passed into the legislation of individual member states, a necessary process before a DIRECTIVE can have effect.

We all know 1992 is coming. The question is when.

Karl Otto Pohl in 1990, when head of the Bundesbank

SITC

See STANDARD INDUSTRIAL TRADE CLASSIFICATION

ALFRED SLOAN

The man described by Lee Iacocca as "the greatest genius ever in the auto business," Alfred Sloan also wrote one of the first great business biographies, *My Years with General Motors,* and was honored by his alma mater (MIT), which named its business school after him.

Between 1923, when he became president of a rather rickety General Motors, and the end of World War II, Alfred Sloan transformed the COMPANY into the largest and most profitable car company in the world. He did it by finding a special balance between central authority and DECENTRALIZATION. While he personally was involved in the selection of every GM executive, he gave those executives considerable power to run their own operations.

One notably contrary view of Sloan and his book has come from James O'Toole, a MANAGEMENT professor who has pointed out that "for the first 300 pages or so, Sloan seems oblivious to the fact that there are any employees in the company. . . . By reading this book [my students] learn which management practices to avoid."

SMALL AND MEDIUM-SIZED ENTERPRISES

The lifeblood of a nation's industry, a fact recognized by most governments through special tax rates and through special agencies (such as the Small Business Administration) set up to provide soft loans and other support services to small and medium-sized ENTERPRISES.

ADAM SMITH

Eighteenth-century author of *The Wealth of Nations* and inventor of the "invisible hand," the idea that free markets ensure that the pursuit of self-interest produces benefits for all. His theories were popular with Thatcherites and Reaganites in the 1980s.

All wealth springs from the Earth.

Adam Smith

Software

The opposite of HARDWARE. Those bits of a COMPUTER that are generally invisible; the bundle of electronic messages, for example, that make up a computer PROGRAM, without which hardware is useless.

Sole proprietor

If you cannot found a COMPANY, then a PARTNERSHIP will do. If you cannot find a partner, then God bless you. Because you will have to be a sole proprietor, like small shopkeepers who trade only on their own account. They may have employees, but whatever PROFIT they make at the end of the day is all theirs.

Sources and uses of funds

An accounting statement showing the cash coming in and the cash going out of a COMPANY during a year—that is, the alterations in its WORKING CAPITAL.

Span of control

The optimum number of subordinates over whom a manager can exercise CONTROL. In 1933 a MANAGEMENT consultant, V. Graicunas, attempted to demonstrate mathematically that it is impossible to exercise proper control over any more than six individuals.

Most consultants since agree that "it depends on the six." Some chief executives have been found to exercise direct control over more than 20 staff members without any apparent loss of efficiency. Others seem to find even one overwhelming.

Special promotion

A MARKETING term for an exceptional offer of a new or revived product. This can come in a number of different guises. For example, it can be in the form of a price DISCOUNT for a limited period of time, it can consist of a heavily advertised contest giving away the product as prizes, or, more modestly, it can be a special window display appearing in a conspicuous department store.

Whatever form it takes, a special promotion (if successful) requires that production schedules be temporarily adjusted. Its aim is to create an exceptional level demand in order to introduce new customers to a product.

SPECIFICATION

The detailed description of an article and the way it is to be produced, given by a buyer to a supplier. Sometimes called "spec": "This sample is not according to spec."

SPOT CHECK

An unannounced random check to see that work is being done correctly. It can be used as a technique of QUALITY CONTROL, but only as part of a wider system of checking. A spot check may fall on one of the few articles well produced, or, probably, on one of those few badly produced.

SPREADSHEET

A type of COMPUTER PROGRAM particularly useful in aspects of business such as planning, budgeting, or investment APPRAISAL. It enables the user to change one variable in a string of complicated mathematical relationships and have the computer roll out the effect on all the other variables. This is much appreciated, for example, when you have just planned and COSTED a DIRECT MAIL operation, and the post office comes up with an entirely new price structure.

STAKEHOLDER

This refers to the wide range of "constituencies" that have a "stake" in a corporation's activities. These constituencies range from suppliers to employees to customers to government. They also include shareholders.

At different times in business history, and in different industrial societies, certain stakeholders have gained power and influence at the expense of others. In the United Kingdom and the United States the shareholder has been king for some time; the customer a mere incidental. In Japan the situation is exactly the reverse. In both cases there are imbalances between stakeholders that must be corrected.

STANDARD DEVIATION

A basic statistical measure of the extent to which a series of data spreads out from a central core figure. This is important for managers as a tool to help them judge, for example, how far sales (or interest rates) might rise or fall in future business cycles based on the extent of their deviation from a norm (or "standard") in the past.

STANDARD INDUSTRIAL TRADE CLASSIFICATION

A widely used system of numbering industrial sectors, subsectors, and individual products. Particularly useful to government agencies and statisticians, investment analysts, and MARKET researchers.

Standard industrial trade classification (SITC) numbers have six digits: the first two indicate the basic industry; the third gives the industry subgroup; the fourth, the specific industry; the fifth, the product class; and the sixth, the individual product.

STANDARDIZATION

The process of getting rid of variety. This can apply to a production line on which it is more efficient to produce only two "standardized" products instead of 13 or 30. Or it can apply to an industry (or a group of countries like the EUROPEAN COMMUNITY) that agree to certain standards that their products must meet.

Such standards may be applied to the dimensions or contents of the products and may be produced for perfectly sound reasons like safety. They may also be produced for unsound reasons, like the need to find work for idle bureaucrats.

Within the EC the process is more commonly called "harmonization" (see **SINGLE MARKET**).

STARS

One of the categories in the famous **BOSTON MATRIX** classification of companies. Stars are companies in the top right-hand corner of the matrix. They have a large **MARKET SHARE** in a fast-growing sector. They may nevertheless devour great chunks of cash in the short term.

START-UP

A business that is just beginning. "Start-up **COST**" is the money that such a business needs before it begins to trade.

Those involved in start-ups have four main places to look for such money.

- Their own pockets, or those of family and friends
- **COMMERICAL BANKS**
- Government funds
- **VENTURE CAPITAL**

STATISTICS

Any manager should have a fundamental grasp of statistical methodology in order to understand **MARKETS** or productivity. Many people who have an extraordinary ability to grasp complicated intellectual concepts go weak at the knees when presented with lists of numbers or even with graphical representations of those lists.

One of the most important concepts is that of averaging: finding the most typical number out of a particular series of "readings." Say you have counted how many people went into a particular shop every day over a two-week period (rounded off to the nearest ten).

	First Week	Second Week
Monday	60	70
Tuesday	130	110
Wednesday	80	80
Thursday	80	120
Friday	120	130
Saturday	160	150
Sunday	10	closed

There are several averages that can be taken here.

The mean. All the people added together and divided by the number of days: (60 + 130 + 80 + 80 + . . .) divided by 13.

The median. The middle number if all the readings are listed in order: 10, 60, 70, 80, 80, 80, 110, 120, 120, 130, 130, 150, 160. The middle number here is 110.

The mode. The number that occurs most frequently—in this sequence, 80, which occurs on three different days.

Averaging is a way of condensing a lot of information into a single simple number. If you do not wish to lose information in this way, an alternative is to represent the sequence of numbers by a chart. The most common types of charts used in business are:

• A straight-line graph
• A bar chart
• A pie diagram

STOCK MARKET

The first stock markets were places where farmers met to buy and sell their livestock. They are now more usually markets in stocks and SHARES. Traditionally, stock markets had a physical presence in a building called a stock exchange, where traders got together to meet brokers and to deal. Nowadays they increasingly exist over telephone lines, with deals struck between brokers who rarely take their eyes off a COMPUTER screen. They seldom venture into a stock exchange.

October. This is one of the peculiarly dangerous months to speculate in stocks. The others are July, January, September, April, November, May, March, June, December, August, and February.

Mark Twain

STOCK OPTION

See OPTION

STOCKTAKING

The business of recording and counting the amount of inventory held by a COMPANY. This has to be done at least once a year for the annual accounts. But with the help of COMPUTERIZED records of sales and purchases, stocktaking can be a continuous process, with a company able to say at any one moment how much stock it holds. Nevertheless, it will still need to have a physical stocktaking every now and then, if only to check that the goods that it records as being there really are there.

STRATEGIC ALLIANCE

The bringing together of bits of companies in a loose PARTNERSHIP in order to improve the COMPETITIVENESS of both. Strategic alliances are appropriate when full takeovers or mergers are not. They have been particularly popular among Europe's ailing electronics firms as they fight the commercial challenge from Japan and the United States. For example, the Netherlands' Philips and Germany's Grundig agreed to merge their video businesses.

A strategic alliance between two bad businesses, however, is unlikely to make a good one.

> *Great ideas often enter reality in strange guises and with disgusting alliances.*
>
> Alfred North Whitehead

STRATEGIC BUSINESS UNIT

A self-contained part of a business that serves a homogeneous MARKET, that is, bits of business that have been stuck together because they all supply the same sort of customer and can do so better by being together. A strategic business unit (SBU) can cut right across traditional geographical and functional divisions within an organization, and it has been encouraged by the love affair that industry in most countries has been having recently with its customers.

STRATEGIC INTENT

A concept first put forward by two business professors, Gary Hamel and C. K. Prahalad, in a *Harvard Business Review* article of the same name. Strategic intent is the broad long-term objective of a corporation that is often encapsulated in those snappy phrases beloved by the Japanese, such as Komatsu's "Encircle Caterpillar." These objectives act as a lighthouse for everybody in the corporation for years.

STRATEGY

The way in which a corporation decides to set about achieving its future goals.

Two **MANAGEMENT** consultants, Benjamin Tregoe and John Zimmerman, devised a simple 14-part questionnaire that they called the "Strategic IQ Test" to determine how strategy oriented companies are. To how many of the following questions would your **COMPANY** answer "yes"?

- The direction of future organizational development is clearly defined by upper management.
- Each manager knows details of the strategy.
- Each manager agrees on the details of the strategy.
- Each manager has a common view of new products and **MARKETS**, based on the company's strategy.
- The company's strategy is the most important factor in evaluating new opportunities.
- Strategy is developed independently of long-range planning.
- Strategy determines plans and guides resource allocation.
- Strategy is based on analysis and assumptions, not on plans.
- Strategy guides acquisitions and **CAPITAL** expenditure, not the other way around.
- Each division or **SUBSIDIARY** has a clear strategy.
- Each division's strategy is entirely consistent with the overall strategy of the organization.
- Each department has a clear strategy.
- Each department's strategy is entirely consistent with the overall strategy of the organization.
- The organization (and its divisions) are evaluated on the basis of strategic performance as well as operating performance.

The greater the number of "yes" answers, the higher the company's strategic IQ.

STRESS

Stress costs industrialized societies billions of dollars a year in absenteeism, alcoholism, and premature death. Yet industry pays little attention to reducing stress, partly because it is still considered to be a weakness by both employer and employee. It is not something that the ambitious manager wants to admit to.

A small number of companies are beginning to offer counseling and techniques like *shiatsu* and meditation to help their executives cope with stress. Such companies, however, are only on the fringes of industry. Many researchers now believe that stress is rooted in the organization as much as in the individual. They talk of the "damaged organization," and look to companies to heal themselves before they try to heal their employees.

Some of the most common causes of industrial stress are:

- Internal change, particularly due to MERGERS AND ACQUISITIONS
- Social change, as when men take on more domestic responsibilities because wives get jobs outside the home
- Inadequate training to cope with the demands of the job
- A dogmatic MANAGEMENT style with autocratic superiors
- Blocked career opportunities due to rigid career ladders
- An increased workload in an attempt to be more competitive

STRIKE

Strikes started out by being good things. Gold prospectors made lucky strikes in California in 1849. Then they became bad things, occasions when workers refused to work in order to try and force their employers to pay them more. Nowadays such organized withdrawals of LABOR are more euphemistically referred to as "industrial action."

If industrial workers are taking industrial action when they are not working, one wonders what they are doing when they are working.

Duke of Edinburgh

Structure

The business historian Alfred Chandler called his first great book *Strategy and Structure* in which he suggested that all successful companies must have a structure that is determined by their **STRATEGY**, and that therefore fits that strategy. However, Chandler found that where there was no **COMPETITION**, structure did not change to match changing strategy; it only did so if it made a difference competitively.

There are several steps in designing a business's structure.

- Allocating specific tasks to individuals
- Grouping individuals doing similar tasks into specialist departments; for example, **HUMAN RESOURCES**, **PUBLIC RELATIONS**, and so on
- Setting up systems to facilitate communication and coordination between departments
- Allocating responsibilities within each department (see **HIERARCHY**)
- Distributing authority throughout the organization

Subcontractor

A **COMPANY** or individual who agrees to provide goods or **SERVICES** to another company in order to help that company fulfill a **CONTRACT** it has with a third party. The subcontractor has no contract with the third party.

Subsidiary

A **COMPANY** that is controlled by another company, called a holding company. In most cases such **CONTROL** is demonstrated by the holding company owning more than 50% of the subsidiary's **SHARES**.

A company may, however, still be a subsidiary if another company owns less than 50% of its shares but controls the composition of its **BOARD**. A subsidiary of company X is also a subsidiary of any company of which X is, in turn, a subsidiary.

Subsidiary companies are of interest to accountants, who "consolidate" them with their holding companies, and to tax inspectors, who want to be sure that there is no **TAX EVASION** from the inessential shunting of goods between subsidiaries and their holding company.

> *Big companies are small companies*
> *that succeeded.*
>
> Robert Townsend

Subsidize

The giving of money, usually by government, to a **COMPANY** or industry in order to reduce its prices below what they would otherwise be. Governments subsidize industries for various reasons.

- To save jobs a little longer in declining industries, like steel or shipbuilding
- As a form of **PROTECTIONISM** against foreign manufacturers, of things like sugar and apples
- As a way of cultivating new **HIGH-TECH** industries that are struggling to survive
- As a way of ensuring that nationally significant industries, such as aerospace or weapons, do not die out

Succession planning

The task that many people argue is the most important for a chief executive: choosing a successor. Mortimer Feinberg, an expert on the subject, lays down certain guidelines for those who have to make such choices.

- Choose early, disclose late.
- Draw the "invisible" organization chart—that is, the differences between titular equals.
- Identify the "hidden influential" people in the **COMPANY**.
- Spell out the unwritten rules.
- Control the bloodletting.
- Free the successor from restrictive commitments.
- Share your observations about people, but do not impose them.
- Let the successor's credentials speak for themselves; do not overpraise the individual.
- Plunge the newcomer into the deep end.

SUNSET INDUSTRY

An old industry that is dying slowly, often because governments will not allow free-market euthanasia. Such industries are frequently metal based and found near waterway transport.

SUNSHINE INDUSTRY

A young industry that is growing quickly, usually in the **HIGH-TECH** area. The sort of business that is found in science parks on the edge of towns with technologically advanced universities (for example, near Boston; Nice, France; or Cambridge, England).

SWAP

Technically an agreement between two parties to swap their debts so that one meets the interest and **CAPITAL** payments of the other, and vice versa. Such an arrangement can be useful if, for example, one borrower wants to change the currency of its debt. This might make what it owes more proportional to what it is owed.

SYSTEM

The way in which something organizes its own internal procedures, as in COMPUTER system or monetary system. A systems analyst designs programs that make computers perform required tasks. Companies also have systems that need to be redesigned occasionally.

Tactics

A term borrowed from the military; the means whereby a STRATEGY is to be achieved.

Takeover

To take over a COMPANY is simply to gain CONTROL of it. A takeover is a formal process of gaining control that, in the case of public companies, involves procedures dictated by the local stock exchange and/or government. A "hostile takeover" is one that is unwelcome to the company being taken over; a "reverse takeover" is one where the company being taken over successfully defends itself by launching a takeover bid for the company that is bidding for it—in other words, biting back.

Somebody wishing to launch a takeover of a public company makes a bid: an offer to the company's shareholders for their SHARES. The offer includes a price and a deadline, by which time the shareholders must have rejected or accepted the offer.

The price may either be in cash (a "cash offer") or in shares and other SECURITIES of the company making the bid (a "paper offer"). In a cash offer the price must be higher than the quoted price of the shares of the company being bid for. Otherwise shareholders will be better off selling their shares on the STOCK MARKET.

With a paper offer, shareholders have some complicated calculations to make. The VALUE of the shares that they are being offered will fluctuate. When the brewer Guinness bid for the Scotch-maker Distillers, it offered its own shares to Distillers' shareholders. Guinness then contrived artificially (and illegally) to raise its share price so that it would have to give Distillers' shareholders fewer shares.

There are many more takeovers in English-speaking countries—where shares tend to be widely held—than there are elsewhere. Hostile takeovers are hugely disruptive to both the tak-er-over and the taken-over, and cases where they are fully justified in the long term are probably few. In the United States merged companies have been found to lose, on average, about 40% of the joint market share of the premerged companies.

TARGET PRICE

There are two meanings.

1. It is the price that a buyer sets a manufacturer for goods whose COST the manufacturer has been asked to estimate.
2. It is a technical term within the EUROPEAN COMMUNITY'S Common Agricultural Policy for the price fixed from time to time by the EC for agricultural goods. It is not a guaran-teed price that farmers will get, but an estimate of what would be a fair price for them.

TARIFF

A tax on imported goods, usually expressed as a percentage of the VALUE of the goods. Under a series of so-called rounds of the GATT, countries have gradually agreed over the last few de-cades to reduce their tariffs.

Many countries, however, still impose high tariffs on certain categories of imports, such as textiles. Their aim is less to raise revenue for the government than to protect domestic industries from foreign COMPETITION.

TAX AVOIDANCE

This is the legal practice of making tax bills as small as possible. Tax authorities have no obligation to show taxpayers (be they individuals or corporations) how to pay a minimum amount of tax. On the other hand, no taxpayer is obliged to pay more than the minimum due.

This has led to a huge industry in tax advice. Advisers can make taxpayers aware of tax allowances that are only available if actually claimed. They can also suggest ways of channeling income from different parts of the world into "tax havens": countries or areas of countries with low tax rates and (usually) little else.

The whole tax-avoidance business is unproductive, and it adds nothing to the wealth of nations. Ideally it too should be avoided by the imposition of simple-to-collect and simple-to-calculate taxes instead of complicated things like corporation tax, a tax that raises very little revenue for considerable cost.

TAX EVASION

The illegal practice of not paying taxes by making false declarations of income or CAPITAL.

FREDERICK TAYLOR

The highly influential inventor of "scientific management," Taylor was a talented man. He won the U.S. doubles tennis championship in 1881, and he was a prolific inventor.

Scientific management was deeply rooted in the nineteenth century. Obsessed with measurement (all the foremen in Taylor's factories had stopwatches), Taylor created a framework for studying labor, but it almost completely ignored the human element in labor.

TEST MARKETING

The launch of a new product on to a restricted MARKET to test the public's response before incurring the full COST of launching nationally or internationally. For CONSUMER goods, test marketing is often done in regions covered by a single commercial television network.

THEORY X

One extreme on a spectrum of views about humans' attitudes to work. Theory X and THEORY Y were expounded by Douglas

McGregor, a social psychologist who was professor of MANAGE-
MENT at MIT for a decade from the mid-1950s.

Theory X is the traditional view of things: humans have a
natural aversion to work and will avoid it if they can. Therefore
they have to be coerced and threatened to get them to do things.
Managers who take this view generally get a hostile reaction
from employees, which reinforces their original view.

THEORY Y

This is the other side of McGregor's THEORY X. It proposes that
humans naturally find work satisfying, and that MANAGEMENT
systems built on that assumption will give individuals responsibility and freedom to attain the corporation's objectives under
their own steam.

Most criticisms of Theory Y are based on its failure to take
account of the fact that many people fall far short of being self-
motivating, creative individuals.

TIME AND MOTION

A system for measuring the speed and efficiency at which a
worker operates in order both to improve them and to set standards for other workers to meet.

Time and motion "studies" are now out of fashion, belonging
to an industrial age when the distinction between humans and
machines was less well appreciated.

TIME MANAGEMENT

The way in which individual managers organize the use of their
own time; a favorite subject for checklists. Here is one.

• Plan each day the night before.
• Make a list of tasks in order of priority, and work out the
  time needed for each.
• Isolate the key tasks, and make sure that they get done.

- Do not clutter the day with tasks that can wait.
- Build in time for solitude, or for an unpredictable problem that could arise.
- Reduce interruptions from phone calls and so on at times earmarked for tasks.
- Relate each day to the rest of the week, month, and so on, and to your goals.

TIME SHEET

A card on which is recorded the hours worked by employees each day in order to calculate their weekly wages. The wages will normally be based on a certain minimum number of working hours, anything above them being paid at OVERTIME rates.

TOTAL QUALITY MANAGEMENT

The idea that quality is something that must be disseminated throughout an organization and not just left to a quality "controller" who examines goods as they emerge at the end of a production line (when it is too late to do much about them).

In 1988 a group of top European executives formed a loose-knit organization called the European Foundation for Quality Management (EFQM). Its purpose was to propagate the idea of total quality management (TQM) across Europe.

The EFQM says that TQM strategies are characterized by the following.

- EXCELLENCE of all managerial, operational, and administrative processes
- A culture of continuous improvement in all aspects of the business
- An understanding that quality improvement results in cost advantages and better profit potential
- The creation of more intensive relationships with customers and suppliers

- The involvement of all personnel
- Market-oriented organizational practices

Quality is representative of a culture which we Europeans have no reason to let others monopolize. The Europe of Descartes, the Europe of the Age of Reason and the Enlightenment, the Europe of the industrial and technological revolution of the last two centuries holds within itself all the elements of method and exactitude conveyed by the term "total quality."

Raymond Levy, president of Renault

TQM

See **TOTAL QUALITY MANAGEMENT**

TRADE BARRIER

Something that discourages the free flow of trade. The most obvious barriers to trade are import duties (a percentage tax on imports) and quotas (a quantitative ceiling on the volume of imports). As the GATT forces more and more countries (often reluctantly) to dismantle these barriers, they erect a growing number of "invisible" barriers in their place.

The Japanese are alleged to be past masters at the erection of invisible barriers. Theirs range from the Byzantine nature of their distribution system, which works against naive importers, to the simple fact that the Japanese **CONSUMER** is averse to things that are not made in Japan (unless it be a Louis Vuitton handbag).

TRADEMARK

The special mark that a manufacturer puts on its products to distinguish them from those of other manufacturers. The camel on a packet of cigarettes is one example.

Trademarks can be registered so that nobody else can use them legally without permission. Nevertheless, they are frequently stolen by counterfeiters. Yves St. Laurent estimates it loses $60 million a year from sales of fake bottles of its perfume.

TRADE UNIONS

Organizations formed by a group of workers who get together to use the power of COLLECTIVE BARGAINING to improve their lot. Workers pay a fee to the union to become members, and the union then negotiates pay and conditions with employers on their behalf. Unions organize STRIKES and support their members while they are on strike (and unpaid).

Many unions are organized according to the craft of their members (electricians, printers), but some are organized by industry (banking, coal mining), and some consist only of the employees of a single firm. In such cases they are usually referred to as staff associations. There are country variations.

Trade could not be managed by those who manage it if it had so much difficulty.

Samuel Johnson

TRAINING

Teaching employees new knowledge or skills so they can do their current jobs better or so they can move to other jobs within the same organization.

Companies set about training employees in many different ways. The very biggest have their own training centers where staff are sent from time to time. The accounting and MANAGE-MENT consulting firm Arthur Andersen has a vast training center near Chicago that is almost like an in-house university for all Andersen's employees around the world. It has a research center and acts as the guardian of Andersen's CORPORATE CULTURE. Big HIGH-TECH companies like Boeing and IBM spend up to 3.5% of their total sales on training.

Some companies bring in specialist trainers to teach particular skills but rely on in-house trainers for the rest of the time. Others send employees to professional trainers' courses or sponsor them on formal education programs like the MBA. Yet other companies give employees no training whatsoever.

TRANSFER PRICING

The practice of shifting a PROFIT from one country (with a high tax rate) to another (with a low tax rate); transfer pricing skirts on the boundary between TAX AVOIDANCE and TAX EVASION.

Before governments clamped down on transfer pricing it was popular with multinationals. One SUBSIDIARY (in country A) would charge another subsidiary (in country B) a higher-than-market price for an intragroup purchase of goods or SERVICES. That would make no difference to the multinational's overall profit, but it would shift more of it to country B and less to country A, which is nice if country B has a lower CORPORATION TAX rate than country A.

TROUBLESHOOTER

A person sent into a COMPANY for a short period to sort out a particular problem. Troubleshooters are valued for the "fresh eye" that they can bring. Unlike MANAGEMENT consultants, they can remedy the problems they identify themselves.

One description of an ideal troubleshooter from a firm that supplies them is as follows:

A troubleshooter, or crisis manager, is typically aged 40 or older, has at least 10 years of board-level management experience and is able to gain a rapid insight into how a business works at all levels and across all functions, such as marketing, production and finance. He or she also needs to be a good communicator, creative and flexible, as well as mentally and physically tough enough to cope with the stresses of rescuing a company.

The firm that wrote this job description says it receives 2,000 applications from potential troubleshooters every year, but fewer than 1% of them are accepted. It is amazing that it finds so many.

Turnkey project

A large-scale project (such as the building of a new FACTORY or ship) where the contractor agrees to see to every single detail of the construction. The buyer only has to "turn the key" when the project is handed over.

Undercapitalized

The common situation of a **COMPANY** that has too little **CAPITAL** for the amount of business that it is doing, or that it is setting out to do. (See also **OVERTRADING**)

Unique selling proposition

Once upon a time, all good **MARKETING** people would say, "Woe betide the new product that is without a USP." A unique selling proposition (USP) was to a product what "star quality" was to a Hollywood hopeful: absolutely necessary for success, but not sufficient.

A product's USP is the range of unique features that differentiate it from its competitors and that can be conveyed to **CONSUMERS** in a simple **ADVERTISING** message. Marketing people, however, soon discovered that uniqueness is a rare quality, and that it is too much to hope to find it in every new product. So uniqueness gave way to comparison: differentiation from its competitors according to the product's position on a scale of qualities.

Upmarket

A **MARKETING** term describing the higher-price end of the spectrum of a market. Whether to move upmarket is an important strategic issue for many companies. Should they continue to sell low-priced, low-**VALUE**-added goods where **COMPETITION** is increasingly fierce, or should they change to higher-value goods, selling less of them but making more **PROFIT** on each unit sold? In fashion, food, and electronics, companies move upmarket almost constantly.

In a few instances companies decide on the opposite strategy. The Pierre Cardin business, for example, was once a high-fashion French label. Then it decided to stick its name on all sorts of "popular" **DOWNMARKET** products with considerable success.

User-friendly

A term applied to **COMPUTERS** that are easy to use or that provide their user with clear instructions. Nowadays manufacturers aim to make their machines accessible to all.

USP

See **UNIQUE SELLING PROPOSITION**

Value

As in "He is a man who knows the price of everything and the value of nothing." Value is a subjective measure of worth: what something is worth to its owner. That may be more than the price tag says it costs (as, say, in the case of jewelry received on special occasions), or it may be less (as in the case of the "free" airline ticket that demands the traveler stay in a particular expensive hotel on arrival).

MARKETING can be described as the art of making CONSUMERS feel that they have at least got "value for money"; that is, the product (and all its associations) is worth to them at least as much as they paid for it.

Value-added tax

A simple-to-collect tax imposed on consumption. Popular in Europe, value-added tax (VAT) is imposed at every stage of the production process. It is paid by the purchaser of goods and SERVICES and is levied as a percentage of the selling price. Manufacturers pay VAT on their input and then charge it on their sales. They hand over to the government the tax that they have collected, net of the tax that they have paid. So the IRS ends up, in effect, collecting the tax on the VALUE added at each stage of the manufacturing process. Yet the burden of paying the tax actually falls on the CONSUMER.

Different rates of VAT apply to different goods and services. Some things, like books and children's clothes, may be "zero-rated" (that is there is no VAT on them at all). Within the EUROPEAN COMMUNITY strenuous efforts are being made to harmonize rates of VAT, and what is or is not zero-rated.

Value chain

The interlinking activities carried out within a corporation. Identifying those activities and learning how to perform them more cheaply or better than their competitors is the way for a **COMPANY** to gain advantage, according to Michael Porter in *Competitive Advantage: Sustaining Superior Performance* (1985).

VAT

See **VALUE-ADDED TAX**

VENTURE CAPITAL

Synonymous in most dictionaries with **RISK CAPITAL**, venture capital is money for starting new companies or for building up young ones. It is subject to an unusually high degree of risk, and it is expected that most of its return will come from capital gain, not **DIVIDEND** income.

Venture-capital funds, which invest in a portfolio of ventures, expect to find a very few big winners and a large number of big duds. There were fewer duds and more winners in the 1980s than there are today.

On one estimate, only about 12% of all so-called venture capital invested in Europe was going into business **START-UP** by the end of the 1980s: 42% was going into the expansion of existing businesses, and 38% was going into the **MANAGEMENT** buy-out of existing firms (often family-owned firms with succession problems).

The level of venture capital going into start-ups in the United States, especially in **HIGH-TECH** industries, has been generally higher than in Europe. But then U.S. high-tech start-ups have a much higher success rate than European ones.

VERTICAL INTEGRATION

The combining within one organization of groups of operations that follow each other sequentially. For instance, if a **COMPANY** that makes cars buys the company that supplies it with headlights, the car company is involved in backward vertical integration. If the car company buys a chain of car retailers, it is engaged in forward vertical integration.

Vision

Something beyond optical perception that enables one manager to anticipate and avoid commercial disaster while another (without it) trips and falls. Vision is built on imagination, and imagination is in short supply in business life.

Vorstand

The **MANAGEMENT BOARD** in Germany's system of two-tier boards (see *AUFSICHTSRAT*). Members of the *Vorstand* cannot be members of the *Aufsichtsrat*, and vice versa. *Vorstand* members are appointed for fixed terms of office and deal with the day-to-day **MANAGEMENT** of the **COMPANY**.

WAGE FREEZE

The halting by government of increases in wages in order to control INFLATION. This is done in the belief that wages and prices are so closely linked that freezing one must have a similar effect on the other. While wage freezes may slow down the pace of wage increases, they never freeze them altogether, if only because there are always a large number of exceptions, and an equally large number of loopholes.

MAX WEBER

A German professor of law and a social scientist who studied the nature of organizations. He was one of the first to attempt to classify different types of organization, and he noted three.

- The charismatic organization, in which a single leader drives everybody on with his VISION and enthusiasm. This is the style of many religious organizations; it is also the style of the entrepreneurial young business.

- The traditional organization, older and more stable, with an emphasis on traditional ways of doing things. Here accumulated culture is important. Large, well-established multinationals fall into this category.

- The rational/legal organization where everybody has a clearly designated role to play, and where there is a rigid rule book. Such organizations include the military and companies modeled on the military.

WHITE-COLLAR WORKER

A person who arrives at work with a white collar and its standard accompaniment, the tie. Why has such an uncomfortable combination become the standard uniform of MANAGEMENT (except in a few progressive companies like Levi Strauss)? (See BLUE-COLLAR WORKER)

WHITE GOODS

Originally white household goods like sheets and towels. The expression has been taken over by MARKETING people to refer more specifically to white electrical household goods such as refrigerators and washing machines. To be contrasted with BROWN GOODS.

Manufacturers that make white goods tend to diversify into manufacturing other white goods, and likewise for brown goods. It is rare to find the same COMPANY making both white and brown goods, although the Dutch firm Philips is one exception.

WIP

See WORK-IN-PROCESS

WITHHOLDING TAX

Tax that is withheld at source and paid directly to the government without ever passing through a taxpayer's hands. Income tax is withheld at source by many employers from wages and salaries. Tax on interest and DIVIDEND income is often withheld by financial institutions, especially on payments to nonresidents. OFFSHORE financial centers thrive on serving people who do not want their taxes thus withheld.

WORKER PARTICIPATION

Worker participation involves employees in some or all of the following:

- They are allowed and encouraged to own shares in the company they work for.
- They are represented on the BOARD.
- They have access, as a right, to information about their company.
- They have some CONTROL over the MANAGEMENT of their own pension fund.

- They have access to exactly the same facilities—car parks, toilets, and so on—as so-called management.

Worker participation is an attempt to bridge the gap between the white-collar manager and the **BLUE-COLLAR WORKER**.

WORKING CAPITAL

The difference between a **COMPANY'S** current **ASSETS** and its current **LIABILITIES**, that is, the amount of cash it has free and available to run the business. Current assets include easily sellable goods, cash, and bank deposits. Current liabilities include debts due in less than a year, interest payments, and so on. The classic solution to a shortage of working capital is a visit to the bank.

WORK-IN-PROCESS

This includes all the semifinished goods and **SERVICES** in a business, things on their way from being **RAW MATERIALS** and supplies to becoming finished products. Firms try to reduce expensive work-in-progress (WIP) to a minimum. By introducing JIT systems at one factory, Hewlett-Packard cut its WIP from 22 days' worth to one day's worth.

For many companies (like contractors) almost all their **ASSETS** consist of work-in-process, so valuing this unfinished business is very significant in any estimation of such a **COMPANY'S** worth. But how can you **VALUE** things like a half-built hotel?

WORKSTATION

A configuration of **COMPUTERS** that stands alone on an individual's desk and can complete required tasks (such as word processing, spreadsheet work, and so on) without access to a **NETWORK**.

WORK-TO-RULE

A technique used by workers in industrial disputes. They refuse to do any **OVERTIME**, stick rigidly to the **COMPANY'S** rule book, and generally waste time.

WRONGFUL DISMISSAL

Firing an employee for a reason that is not sufficient to justify such extreme action. The law protects employees against what was once common practice. If wrongful dismissal can be proved in the courts, the victim has a right to compensation.

From the idea of wrongful dismissal has come the concept of "constructive dismissal." In this case an employee is treated by an employer in such a way (unjustifiably demoted or victimized without actually being fired) that he or she has the right to resign and claim wrongful dismissal.

Yield

In general this refers to the output of any of the factors of production (land, **LABOR**, and **CAPITAL**). Thus yield can refer to the wheat produced per year per acre from a particular plot of land, or it can refer to the tons of coal dug up by a single miner in a year.

It is most commonly used with reference to the annual return (the output) from an investment of capital. An investment of $1,000 that produces $90 in a year has a yield of 9%. This sort of yield comes in several forms.

DIVIDEND yield. The annual pre-tax amount that shareholders receive as dividend, expressed as a percentage of the amount they invested.

Earnings yield. The pre-tax **PROFITS** of a **COMPANY** (its "earnings") divided by the number of **SHARES**, expressed as a percentage of the price per share. This is the reciprocal of the **P/E RATIO**.

Flat yield. The yield taking into account only the income earned on an investment; the sort of yield obtained from a bank deposit where the capital sum does not change from the moment it is made to the time it is withdrawn.

Gross/net yield. The yield expressed before/after tax is paid.

Redemption yield. A yield that takes into account any capital gain (or loss) to be made on the redemption of an investment. This is particularly useful in calculating the return to be made on fixed-interest **SECURITIES** (like government **BONDS**). These are issued with a fixed rate of interest and then sold in the secondary **MARKET** at a **DISCOUNT** or at a premium to their "redemption price," depending on whether current market rates are higher or lower than their fixed rate.

ZAIBATSU

The large groups of Japanese financial and industrial companies that are interlinked by cross-shareholdings and long-term commercial links. Such groups include Mitsubishi, Sumitomo, and Mitsui. A more modern name for these groups is "keiretsu," which means "headless combines."

Many have attributed Japan's industrial success to the existence of the zaibatsu, but others argue that the fastest-growing Japanese companies of the past two decades have been firms like Toyota, Sony, and Canon, none of them part of a zaibatsu.

ZERO-BASE BUDGETING

A popular way of drawing up budgets that assumes that there was no budget at all last year. Managers are asked to justify *all* expenditure each year. They are not allowed to get away with justifying only the increase. In practice, zero-base budgeting (ZBB) is time-consuming and difficult to implement, but the idea that no expenditure should ever be taken for granted is a healthy one.

ZERO DEFECT

Some Japanese companies have the audacious ambition to produce goods that have no faults whatsoever. Few if any achieve it, but if none of them had the ambition, then for sure none of them would achieve it.